Finish Strong!

Love,

Eph 2:10

The Back Nine

Sherry Bradshaw

THE BACK NINE

ISBN:
TRADE PAPERBACK: 978-1-939779-35-9
HARDBACK: 978-1-939779-36-6

Published by

LIFEBRIDGE
BOOKS
P.O. Box 49428
Charlotte, NC 28277

Dedication

In finishing this book, I have found that it has been all about the process and not the final product. God has taught me so much through writing The Back Nine—Finishing Strong. However, just because I am on the Back 9 doesn't mean I don't still have things to learn! I have truly enjoyed putting this project together because it is in the "process" that we grow—that we take some of our most "important" life shots as God refines, teaches, and develops us.

One of my favorite parts of writing a book is the dedication. It causes me to realize that nothing happens on our own. Success is not "an individual." I would not be where I am today without the people who have had a major impact on my life.

To my husband's parents, Charlie and Judy. They have done the unthinkable in their Back 9 by having to bury their baby girl, Dargan, when she was just 47. We all love and miss her every day. They are currently enduring watching their oldest son, Charlie, battle throat cancer. We are all praying for his complete healing. He is a champion. They have taught me many lessons, but the most important one so far is how to lean heavily on the Lord and trust when you don't understand. Watching them continue to "press on," finishing strong, has spoken volumes to me.

To Leslie, my Back 9 blog editor. You are God's angel sent from heaven above. I couldn't do any of this without you.

To Mike, our daughter's boyfriend of five years. I am so thankful for the love, respect, and commitment you have given to Collins, especially through the massive storms in her life. For being strength and support for her and pursuing your relationship with our Lord. You are loved and appreciated.

To Logan. You are such a precious soul who is truly making your shots count.

To Collins—for just being you, my sunshine, my sidekick, my little partner in all the girly stuff we love. I am so very blessed to have a daughter. You are the best! Thank you for loving Jesus.

To Brewer and Thomas—my "dream team." Thank you for the strong men you are. For loving and deeming family important. Seek Christ, my boys, in all you do.

To Charlie, Virginia, Mary Pat, Whitt, Julia, and Francis. You are simply the best.

To Marcia, Timmy, Tucker, and Lauren—Sweet Papa—Papa Sam and Aunt Joellen. You have served and supported me for years. Your generosity and love humbles me daily. Thanks for loving me unconditionally. I love you all so much. You are my roots.

To Bill, my husband. Hang with this "crazy lady" in the Back 9. I feel the best is yet to come. We will finish strong.

To my beloved mother who is now with the Lord. For teaching me throughout your life that "This is the day the Lord has made—rejoice and be glad in it!" I cannot wait to reunite with you one day.

Finally, to Jesus—my Rock, my Fortress, my All in All. To You I give all the honor, and the praise. My desire is to Finish Strong for Your glory!

"Even when I am old and gray, do not forsake me, my God, till I declare Your power to the next generation, Your mighty acts to all who are to come" (Psalm 71:18).

Contents

INTRODUCTION

God definitely has a sense of humor when He takes someone like me who has been a cheerleader and dancer for the first part of the "Front 9" of life and then bestows upon me three children who all chose golf as their sport of choice. All three, two boys and one girl, played golf at a highly competitive level with one turning professional. This cheerleader/mother has had to "tone it down."

Cheering on the golf course is defined as whispering, not screaming. Did I mention that dancing is NOT allowed on the course? There was once, just once, that I had to ignore the rules. It may have embarrassed my kids and other spectators, but I had to bust a move!

Please understand: this mother knew nothing of golf, had never played the sport nor been a member of a country club until my husband and I had children. Not only did I have to learn hundreds of rules so that I could fully understand the game, but golf also requires a dress code for spectators. I don't know of another sport that demands so much from the fans on the sidelines.

God's plan is always perfect. Becoming a "golfer mom" has taught me, stretched me, shaped me, and refined me. I have found that the game truly does parallel much of our walk—especially in the Christian life.

In golf, every shot counts. The Back 9 of a golf course

often represents an opportunity to improve your score. You have already played 9 holes and had a chance to learn the speed of the greens, adjusted to the weather conditions, become comfortable with your playing partners, among other things. These are factors that should help a golfer improve his or her game. So it is in life. On the Back 9, you are making the turn. You have lived a little and experienced a "learning curve." We all gain wisdom and knowledge by doing, by falling, by getting up, and by learning from others. It is what we choose to do with what we have absorbed that is key to finishing strong.

I marvel over a curiosity I discovered about the Back 9 and a solid finish. All three of our kids were always more satisfied with their round when they played the Back 9 well! If they had an excellent Front 9 but somehow had a letdown on the back, it truly stole some of the joy out of their round. However, if they didn't have a great Front 9 but found their game on the Back 9—made some birdies and finished well—it made all the difference in how they felt about their performance. When they finished strong, they were the most pleased and satisfied.

I have noted this same phenomenon with countless other golfers. It's amazing how much happier they are if they finish well, regardless of their total score. In life, I do believe it is how you finish! No one wants to begin strong and end weak!

On life's journey, all of our shots are important. Romans 14:12 states, *"So then, each of us will give an account of ourselves to God."*

Yes, we are all going to sign a "scorecard" which is a record for all the shots we make in life. The great news is that salvation is a "free gift." It is not about your best drive or putt—not about *what* you grip but *Who* you grip? This is why I encourage you to hold tightly to Jesus as your Lord and Savior. Then your walk is about allowing God to be your perfect "Caddy" for making your shots truly significant. He knows all the exact yardages, and the right club to pull. He knows where the trouble is and how to avoid the hazards. He will even repair your "ball marks."

If you read my earlier book, *The Front Nine,* you know that the first "tees" were: #1 Dreams, #2 Your DNA, #3 Relationships, #4 Choices, #5 Mistakes, #6 Adversity, #7 Confidence, #8 Expectation, and #9 Tomorrow. So now, as we make "the turn," we move to the last half of the course, starting on Tee #10.

No matter what hole you find yourself on, if you are breathing, know that God is not dead and He is not finished with you! Please open your heart and mind as you read this book and allow God to be your "Caddy" and help you make shots that count for eternity, not just for your days here on earth!

I believe what you are about to learn on *The Back Nine* will help you finish strong.

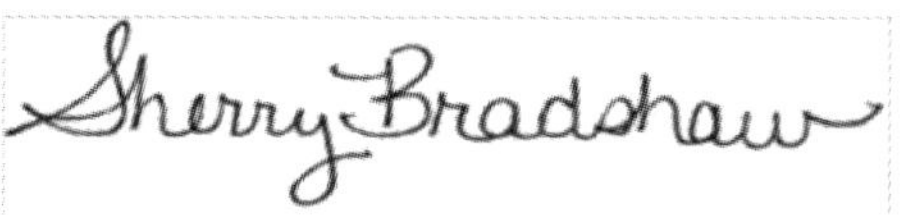

TEE #10

POSSIBILITIES

It was rather amazing that a girl from a small town in the western foothills of South Carolina could make it to the Miss America Pageant, especially with a talent practically no one had heard of.

If you read *The Front Nine,* you know that I began "clogging" at the age of ten. It became a passion of mine and I was named World Clogging Champion four years in a row. After graduating from Clemson University, I entered the Miss South Carolina competition and won—with clogging as my talent.

Then it was on to Atlantic City for the Miss America Pageant. This toe-tapping, knee-slapping folk dance of the Appalachian mountains was in my blood.

Along the way, I learned many valuable principles I want to share with you. I pray you will awaken to the truth, as I have, that if you are in God's will, even when you lose, you win—and that the Lord's comfort far outweighs life's disappointments. I also want you to discover how to tap into insights and possibilities that will help you meet every challenge.

Now that I'm on the "back nine," I have great memories of my clogging days, but I realize I might find myself stuck in some crazy position or hurt if I tried to demonstrate dance moves that were once second nature!

I remember like it was yesterday when the judges interviewed me in Atlantic City. Actress Cicely Tyson asked, "What on earth is clogging?"

There had been a lot of hype by the press that my feet would "dazzle" and "crank up" the audience. So this Southern girl had a lot of expectations to live up to.

At the Friday dress rehearsal, I was shocked as I walked out on stage and was surrounded by cameras, and hundreds of people waiting to see me perform.

I thought I was prepared, but the glare of the limelight caught me off guard. When the music began, I missed my cue, started late, tried to catch up with my routine and fell—not once, but twice!

That was it; there were no "do-overs!" I walked off the stage in tears, thinking I had disappointed everyone and considered my presentation to be a complete flop.

In retrospect, botching the rehearsal was the best thing that could have happened to me. In the car, while being driven back to the hotel, I was motivated more than ever. I decided that I was going to dance better that night than I had ever danced in my life.

The rest of the afternoon I prayed and rehearsed my routine in my head.

I saw myself starting on time, hitting every step on cue, and how I would move from side to side across the stage. I not only saw the possibilities, but I saw success.

A sports psychologist would call this "visualization."

That night, I gave it everything I had. The fire in my bones had never felt hotter. I had danced on stage literally hundreds of times, in front of hundreds of people, but this evening was by far the most important dance of my life! The audience was rocking and everyone started clapping to the beat of the music, "Are You From Dixie?" Mission accomplished!

When my performance was over, as I left the stage, the cheerleader in me surfaced and I threw a huge "fist pump!"

I was running on an emotional high until they announced the talent winner—and it wasn't me. It was Joanna Fitzgerald, Miss Texas, who electrified the crowd with her "fiddle!" I must admit that she was very deserving, but I was sooooo disappointed!

I struggled with my thoughts in preparing for the final and most important night. All that day I refused to allow doubt to creep into my mind—and did not second guess anything I had done up to that point.

WHAT NEXT?

As a 23-year-old, my faith was strong, and I knew God had me there for a purpose, no matter what others speculated.

My life verse at the time was Proverbs 3:5-6, *"Trust in the Lord with all your heart, and lean not on your own understanding; in all your ways acknowledge Him, and He shall direct your paths."*

I clung to that passage and tried my best to live by its truth, acknowledging God even through the tears of falling in dress rehearsal, the stress of the media interviews, and the attention that surrounded all the contestants. It was definitely a new level of intensity.

The finalists were eliminated one by one until there were only two contestants left on stage—Miss Mississippi and myself. All I can remember is host Gary Collins saying something about, "We have never had a tie for Miss America before"—and then huddling at the judges' table.

I was announced as "First Runner Up" and was immediately pushed to the side so that the attention could appropriately be placed on, "Our new Miss America, Susan Akin."

First runner up? What did that mean? Second best? No crown? No title? No more chances? Go back home to South Carolina? What next?

Risking "losing to win" in the Miss America Pageant taught me to view every day of life as a "Stage On, Lights On, Cameras Roll" moment—not just a dress rehearsal.

Each new morning is a chance to engage, take a risk, make a difference, and fulfill God's purpose.

You can only live the hours you are given. There was so much I discovered:

- I learned that even when you lose, you "win" because overcoming loss is also part of the Lord's plan.
- I learned that people still loved me and my value to those who truly cared was not in my win/loss tally.
- I learned how greatly God comforts in times of disappointment.
- I learned that working hard and leaving no stone unturned doesn't always guarantee the ultimate earthly reward.

- I learned that even in losing, God allowed many amazing opportunities to come my way that would not have existed otherwise.
- I learned how to get up after falling and try again.
- I learned that the sun always rises the next day and it was time to see the possibilities for new adventures.
- I learned humility.
- I learned to respect and be happy for the winner.

Perhaps the greatest lesson of all was that "winning wasn't everything"—and it was not where the Lord wanted me to find my value.

Sure, we have disappointments, but we can't continually live in a "dress rehearsal" mentality. We must realize that life is not tomorrow, next week, or summer break; it is in the here and now!

As long as we are breathing, God is not finished with us. It is our job to seek the opportunities God puts before us and fulfill His purpose—which can be as simple as smiling and giving someone five minutes of our time when he or she needs a listening ear, helping a stranger load their car, or perhaps stepping back and letting a person walk in front of us.

Even though coming up short in the "Miss America" Pageant was a dream "not realized," a crucial lesson I learned—and would like for you also to claim—is Philippians 1:6, *"Being confident of this, that He who began a good work within you will carry it on to completion until the day of Christ Jesus."*

I took comfort in knowing that *Jesus had my back!* He held my "life yardage book" and that He will take and use every moment for His great purpose, not ours.

If you don't compete, you never have a chance to win. So take a number card and get in the game!

SEEING NEW POSSIBILITIES

If you are a man, you might not agree with the next couple of pages, but read on.

Recently, Collins and I were driving home in the car with Bill on Thanksgiving. We were enjoying telling him of our "agreed insight" on a few relationships that we had both observed at the gathering. Bill's response was, "I just don't see that!"

Let me explain why we could "see" things that he could not! Men are not wired the same as women. I'm so glad God gave us a daughter to further validate the "sight" I sometimes have that Bill doesn't.

We have all heard of "a woman's intuition." It is a reality, not a myth. Intuition is defined as *a direct perception of truth, fact; a keen or quick insight independent of an analysis reasoning process.*

Research on nonverbal communication skills has clearly shown that women are far better at reading and decoding facial expressions and emotions than men. One simple test taken with boys and girls involved viewing an equal number of people and objects. Girls overwhelmingly remembered seeing more people than objects, while the boys remembered observing more objects. (There have been many studies done on this topic.)

Most women can walk into a room and read people rather quickly. They can pick up on who is happy, sad, frustrated, etc., while men take little or no notice at all. The differences are scientific and are based on the way male and female brains work differently!

Many times when females have a "read" on a person or situation, men will ask for a logical explanation for what we perceive. Men, please understand women can't always give one! You may have heard a woman comment, "I don't know why, but I just feel this way." Or, "I have a hunch." She might even say, "I just have a suspicion."

Women are much more often in tune emotionally than men. Males just don't notice the subtle difference that a female's brain is constantly computing.

Louann Brizendine, MD, a neuropsychiatrist and author of *The Female Brain* (and also *The Male Brain*), observes, "Being a woman is like having a giant, invisible antennae that reaches out into the world, constantly aware of the emotions and needs of those around you."

A woman's larger *corpus callosum* and increased volume of white matter combine to give her vast complex conscious and unconscious connections between her right brain and left brain. This amazing design gives her insight into a man's world that men simply aren't sensitive enough to see.

Males, learn to trust and value a female's God-given take on the world and those around them. While women aren't right 100 percent of the time, it is clear that their intuition is truly a reality.

We must not overlook the fact that at creation, God said, "It is not good for the man to be alone. I will make a helper suitable for him" (Genesis 2:18).

These God-created differences allow us to complement and help each other. So, gentlemen, when it comes time to discuss personalities and potential, you might want to listen to the "fairer sex."

FAST, OR SLOW?

Some may disagree, but I love living in the age of "speed" and "quickness." This includes drive-thru banks, fast food chains, UPS overnight, texting, email, GPS—and all the things that can help me shave a few minutes off of my time. You could call them "quick fixes!"

But instant, easy, or convenient can also be dangerous. As much as I love getting things done efficiently, and in a hurry, it is not always the best path to take. There are certain truths God deems best for us to learn at a snail's pace.

I grew up on a farm and am proud of it. In fact, you could look out any window of our house and see cows. When I was young, my sister and I gave them names like "Strawberry" or "Blackberry." And going out into the vegetable garden each summer was like finding hidden treasure.

I would watch my dad plow the soil, then we would spread the seeds and cover them up, or plant the seedlings, and later fertilize, weed, and water.

It seemed like forever before we saw anything sprout. Every day I would go out and check—until eventually there would be tiny green tomatoes, one-inch cucumbers, or short beans peeking out from under the leaves.

What a thrill it was to walk toward the garden and see from a distance that the tomatoes had turned orange or red, and were ready to be picked. The fruit was ripe for harvest!

Now, as an adult, as I put the process into perspective, I realize how long it took and the amount of care that was needed for the end result. It didn't happen overnight!

Many things worth having require patience, self-control, plenty of toil, and an overall "gut check" of why you are doing what you are doing! Given the right combination of nourishment, care, and time, we also produce fruit that blesses our heavenly Father.

I believe in all of us there is either an eagle that is waiting to rise above the clouds or a pig that wants to wallow in the mud. The difference between flying and floundering is whether or not we will fight, improve, and overcome.

Peter Lowe, a motivational guru, says it this way: "The most common trait I have found in successful people is that they conquered the temptation to give up."

Regardless of how long success takes, the word "quit" cannot be in your vocabulary.

Patience can only be learned by being challenged and tested. Learning to reach, seek, and achieve takes time, plus a hunger to grow and improve.

CHOOSE TO SOAR!

Diamonds are stunningly beautiful, and most women look

forward to wearing them on their left hand. But that sparkling jewel didn't originate with luster. A diamond begins as a lump of coal, then it goes through a grueling refining process under tremendous pressure. In the end it sits glimmering on a finger and is admired by many!

Success is available and reachable for everyone. The road is not always straight and smooth, because overcoming obstacles is how we grow and improve. Here's what we can rely upon:

- *"Every word of God is pure; He is a shield to those who put their trust in Him"* (Proverbs 30:5).
- *"What then shall we say to these things? If God is for us, who can be against us?"* (Romans 3:31).
- *"Your word is a lamp to my feet and light to my path"* (Psalm 119:105).
- *" Let your light so shine before men, that they may see your good works and glorify your Father in heaven"* (Matthew 5:16).

It is up to us to see the possibilities and make the right choices. It may take more time than we think, but the journey will be exhilarating—and the benefits are well worth the effort.

Let me share these words by Robert Louis Stevenson: "The man is a success who has lived well, laughed often, and loved much; who has gained the respect of intelligent men and the love of children; who has filled his niche and accomplished his task, who leaves the world better than he found it, whether by an improved poppy, a perfect poem, or a rescued soul; who never lacked appreciation of earth's beauty or failed to express it; who looked for the best in others and gave the best he had."

Could this be written about you?

A Second Set of Eyes

"A picture is worth a thousand words!"

I have heard this phrase many times, and wholeheartedly agree with it. I think it is safe to say that we have all seen pictures of children on television who are living in third world countries and are severely malnourished. From their tears and swollen bellies, we know they are starving. We don't need to listen to the news report.

Or, we can open the pages of a newspaper and see a smiling couple at their wedding. We don't need words to tell us what is happening. We can almost feel the love.

I can remember having a professional photo made several years ago and I didn't like the outcome. After my father-in-law saw it, he said with a smile, "Well, you'd better like it, 'cause it looks exactly like you!"

I stopped and thought a minute. He was right. It *was* me! However, I made some mental notes about my picture and set out to make a few changes.

A single picture tells a story; we just need the "eyes" to see what it is saying.

One afternoon, my husband took a video of our son, Thomas, hitting the ball while in a golf competition, and Thomas sent it to his swing coach. After the round, our son was able to get feedback on a minor problem that he could not see for himself. The end result was that Thomas made the change and, wow, his swing immediately improved.

It often takes a picture, or someone to offer an opinion and put a different set of eyes on what we aren't able to detect.

We must have an open mind and a receptive heart to make the changes that will truly benefit us.

I have become an advocate of Christian counseling. There is still an unspoken stigma associated with seeking professional help. The prevailing thought is that if you need to see a counselor, you must really be "messed up."

Now that I am in the *Back Nine* of life, I firmly believe that if more people would look in the mirror, put down their pride, and seek "another set of eyes," then they just might be able to climb out of the valley they currently reside in. Instead, most men and women avoid rocking the boat, believing whatever they are facing will just get better in time. Or they have the misconception, "I can handle this!"

Let me be clear. The very best "Counselor" is the Holy Spirit. If you are unfamiliar with this terminology, please let me explain. The Holy Spirit is God—part of the Trinity (Father, Son, and Holy Ghost). So when you invite Christ into your life, you receive the Spirit, who comes to dwell inside of you.

Before Jesus ascended back to heaven, He stated, *"If you love Me, keep My commandments. And I will pray the Father, and He will give you another Helper [Counselor], that He may abide with you forever—the Spirit of truth, whom the world cannot receive, because it neither sees Him nor knows Him; but you know Him, for He dwells with you and will be in you"* (John 14:15-17).

The Lord continued, and taught, *"But when He, the Spirit of truth comes, He will guide you into all the truth"* (John 16:13).

With this in mind, I hope you will understand why I would only recommend a Christian counselor. In their practice, they base their advice on knowing that God, the Bible, and prayer are where "truth" resides. The best Christian counselors are professionals who place God above themselves. They listen intently; then direct your attention to Scripture and teach you how to commune with the Lord as you examine your challenge or dilemma. They pose questions that help reveal your shortcomings or areas that, most of the time, we are blind to—or that we deep-down know are there but choose not to "see."

Counseling provides a place of privacy, safety, and accountability, where you can "unpack" your life and have a light shined into deep corners where solutions are needed.

I've gone through this process and have been utterly amazed at how God has used my willingness to be vulnerable. I have not only experienced tremendous growth, but have been able to use these insights to help countless others.

BACK IN THE "FAIRWAY OF LIFE"

Just as Thomas using a video of his golf swing, or me

seeking the guidance of a counselor, the opinions of others can be a watershed moment. But please heed this word of warning. The person you choose, should be one with wisdom and professionalism, who has earned the right to have a voice in your life.

When it's time for self-examination regarding the possibility of making major (or minor) changes, be very cautious about trusting the advice of someone just because they may be your friend. Seek a certified, professional.

If you find yourself sinking into a "deep dark hole," there is help available—but only if you are willing to take a step of faith, kick your pride to the curb, and make the time to embrace change.

Welcome the opportunity to seek another viewpoint. With God at the center, you can definitely return to the middle of the "fairway of life." This will give you a clear shot to the green and help you see the countless possibilities of what the future holds.

ARE YOU TEACHABLE?

From personal experience, please allow me to add this word of caution.

If you are talented or highly gifted in a certain area, you may have a very tough time with being "teachable."Extreme giftedness can deceive you into thinking you no longer have anything else to learn. Age can do that too. The older you become, the more you feel you already know. Age and experience are priceless teachers, but the truth is that there is always more to learn, thus, we all need to develop the willingness to be teachable.

I love the words of Proverbs 26:12: *"Do you see a man wise in his own eyes? There is more hope for a fool than for him."* No matter what season of life we find ourselves in, none of us can claim to know it all. Everyone can continue to develop and grow. Who wants to be known as a "fool"?

Unintentionally, or intentionally, our pride in thinking we know it all can stunt our growth, make us stagnant, and trap us in a life of "status quo"—which has never been God's intent. Jesus declared, *"The thief does not come except to steal, and to kill, and to destroy. I have come that they may have life, and that they may have it more abundantly"* (John 10:10).

I have also found that we can get to a place that is comfortable, routine, and predictable—all of which can lull us into a life of complacency.

On around "Hole 8," I discovered that I had become very lethargic in my learning and, as a result, was personally not growing. Life had become busy and routine. And routine was the invisible "virus" that impeded my learning and led to stunted growth. Thankfully, with God's goodness and the promptings of the Holy Spirit, I began to search for "fresh water" instead of a "stale pond."

When I travel and speak, I often share with people that if we are still breathing, God is not finished with us yet. His desire is for you and me to continually grow and learn, seeking to have more of Him. In order for this to happen, we have to become "comfortable with being uncomfortable."

True growth only takes place when we step up, step out, and actively seek fresh opportunities to learn, grow, and experience new things.

Cultivating a habit of reading has been a key ingredient in prompting new growth in my life. It has encouraged me, expanded my thinking of what is possible, and opened my eyes to blind spots in my own Christian walk. It has fueled my desire to learn, change, progress, and truly grasp the meaning or what Sydney J. Harris observed: "A winner knows how much he still has to learn, even when he is considered an expert by others. A loser wants to be considered an expert by others, before he has learned enough to know how little he knows."

I think when the Bible warns us of being a fool, we can safely say that would be the same as a "loser."

God's definition of a winner is to live "an abundant" life in Him—which means growing, learning, and remaining humble! Being teachable, in the most simple terms, is a willingness to open our minds to new ideas and new ways to take action. Pride prevents that, because it is such a huge roadblock to success and the development of our God-given talent and growth. I love how Stephen Covey expresses this: "It takes humility to seek feedback. It takes wisdom to understand it, analyze it, and appropriately act on it."

Today, open your heart and mind to the fact that God's not finished with you—no matter what your age. Satan can use your past success or failures to limit your growth, but the Lord wants you to use them as part of the learning process.

Each day brings exciting new possibilities. Remain teachable and seek to live a life of "continual significance."

NOTES FOR YOUR SCORECARD

- If you are in God's will, even when you lose, you win.
- Without competing, you will never experience success.
- The Lord's comfort far outweighs life's disappointments.
- The Creator gave us, especially women, the intuition to see insights and possibilities.
- We may be in a hurry, but God has His own timetable.
- Be open to having a "second set of eyes" look at your challenge.
- When seeking professional counsel, make sure you find someone who is certified and biblically based.
- Instead of being "wise in your own eyes," remain humble and teachable.

TEE #11
ATTITUDE

Most Americans know the names LeBron James and Rory McIlroy, but not many have heard of Bob Rotella. Dr. Rotella is not in front of the cameras every day like LeBron and Rory, but he works with both so that they can perform their best when it's show time. His teaching has nothing to do with body mechanics and physical performance, but everything to do with mental performance and psychological attitudes.

Dr. Rotella isn't a shrink per se; rather, he is a well-known, successful, sports psychologist, someone who teaches athletes how to think their way to success. And what does this uber successful mentor say is the death wish for any athlete? Answer: Negativity. He is amazed at how so few sports figures focus on what they're doing right, and instead hammer themselves on what they are doing wrong. Negativity creeps into their mindset, climbs on the couch, and never leaves. But don't be fooled, this doesn't only happen to athletes: sadly, some people choose negativity as a lifestyle.

In one of his presentations, Dr. Rotella made the point that the mind can only possess one thought at a time: "You can't be speaking negative and claim to be thinking positive."

If it is true that we must choose positivity or negativity, then we all must remember this: *Attitude is a choice.*

We are all guilty at times of allowing our emotions to rule our thoughts. However, since feelings are fleeting, unpredictable, and deceiving, they should never be used to drive our decisions. Allow me to help you train yourself to think positively.

On this "tee" you will learn how faith, trust, intention, discipline, and constant self-examination leads to optimism and self-confidence—that I call *Godfidence!* We will also explore the issue of unresolved anger and how to use "God's medicine" for emotional health. Among other principles, you will see how a change of direction begins with a change of attitude.

THE TWO REPORTS

A thought always comes before an action. Always. The choice of a negative attitude can be preceded by several variables—fatigue, sickness, stress, pressure, or hunger, just to name a few. How we perceive these things can ultimately steer us into a downward spiral that leads to terrible thoughts, which will eventually, and more tragically, lead to terrible behavior. But there is another side to the coin.

Looking at the same things and thinking about them differently can lead us to completely different behaviors—behaviors that are absolutely incredible for us. To illustrate this point, we find a marvelous example in the Bible.

The children of Israel were about to enter into a land that God had promised them, but there was an obstacle standing in their way.

The leaders, Moses and Aaron, sent out twelve "spies" (one from each of the tribes) to survey the Promised Land and its inhabitants—the territory God pledged to deliver into the hands of the Israelites.

Of the twelve, ten returned with a tale of fear and woe: *"'We are not able to go up against the people, for they are stronger than we.' And they gave the children of Israel a bad report of the land which they had spied out, saying, 'The land through which we have gone as spies is a land that devours its inhabitants, and all the people whom we saw in it are men of great stature. There we saw the giants...and we were like grasshoppers in our own sight, and so we were in their sight'"* (Numbers 13:31-33).

There were twelve spies, but only Joshua and Caleb came back with a glowing report. *"The land we passed through...is exceedingly good. If the Lord delights in us, then He will bring us into this land and give it to us, 'a land which flows with milk and honey.' Only do not rebel against the Lord, nor fear the people of the land, for they are our bread; their protection has departed from them, and the Lord is with us. Do not fear them"* (Numbers 14:7-9).

Both groups were looking at the same thing—the Promised Land. The negative men saw only the giants and warriors that inhabited the territory (a negative thought) which then led to their decision of remaining where they were instead of taking what was promised to them (a negative action).

The positive men looked at the land and began to imagine all the good things that it could offer to their people. They too saw the giants, but only as minor obstacles that stood in the way of their goals—not as immovable barriers. Now, what was the difference between the two groups?

You might be inclined to say that their thoughts separated them, which is true, but what governed their thoughts is the key ingredient toward becoming a positive person. The optimists had unshakable faith.

They claimed God's promise and, because of this, their belief did not waiver.

What is so amazing, yet, knowing human nature, we should have expected the outcome: the children of Israel chose to believe the negative report and it influenced their actions. As a result, they wandered in the wilderness for the next 40 years, most of them dying along the way, never seeing what God had promised.

It is recorded in Scripture: *"Except for Caleb the son of Jephunneh and Joshua the son of Nun, you shall by no means enter the land which I swore I would make you dwell in"* (verses 30-31).

You see, the other spies lacked faith in the Almighty. They refused to acknowledge and rely on the Lord's character and provision. Instead, they made judgments based on their fear and negativity, and it cost them their lives. God declared, *"But as for you...your children will be shepherds here for forty years, suffering for your unfaithfulness, until the last of your bodies lies in the wilderness"* (verses 32-34 NIV).

Here is the underlying truth about how to think positively: *Faith drives our thoughts. If the object of your faith is strong, then your thoughts can be just as powerful.* That's why negative people seem so unhappy—they don't trust in anything strong enough to give them hope in the end; and an end without hope is simply despair.

A ROARING FLAME

A negative attitude not only impacts your thoughts, but can quickly affect your behavior.

Not long ago I was sitting at a red light and the woman in the car next to me was glancing down—probably reading a text message—and didn't see the light turn green. The driver behind her went *nuts*—honking his horn, rolling down the window, and screaming as he zoomed past her stationary vehicle.

That same morning, in the parking lot of a Publix grocery store, I watched a driver pull in front of someone and take their parking spot. There was a loud, verbal altercation that could not be described as friendly!

Then, in the afternoon, I witnessed the impatience and anger of a lady (mid-twenties) as she berated an elderly person who was attempting to write a check in line at Chick-fil-A!

By the time I returned home from my day of errands, I felt exhausted and thought, *What is this world coming to?*"

Anger is an invisible fire! While we see its outward expression, the flame is roaring on the inside.

This problem seems to be gaining a strangle-hold on society. I have a hard time watching certain news shows because the guests constantly try to interrupt and "out-yell" each other to make their point. It's a growing concern, and either people are unaware of what they are doing, or just don't care.

This lack of control over how we conduct ourselves is certainly not new. Long ago, King Solomon said that it is better to meet a mother bear robbed of her cubs than encounter an angry person (see Proverbs 17:12).

Thankfully, the only time I have ever been up close and personal to a bear was when it was caged! On television or in movies, I've seen them provoked, but Proverbs lets us know how dangerous and threatening they can be.

I know how a mother bear feels, because when someone hurts my kids with actions or words, *beware!* It steams me from the inside out!

Once, when I heard that a teacher had used one of our sons as a negative example in a classroom (for no valid reason), it took me a week to get over it. I finally had to take a deep breath, step back, and ask myself, "Why am I still so upset?"

It was because the incident was the straw that broke the camel's back. I was living with unresolved anger over many *other* things and the lack of peace in my spirit was like "a smoldering fire" that suddenly erupted into a raging inferno.

When verbal attacks present themselves, it is because far too many haven't taken time to apply the message, *"A fool vents all his feelings, but a wise man holds them back"* (Proverbs 29:11).

I've had to address the issue with myself, and also with our children.

Let me share eight answers for dealing with anger:

1. You have to pray!

Ask God for His help and the strength to deal with anger. We are seldom capable of handling it on our own.

2. You must confront the issue.

Ignoring the problem is like failing to treat a wound; it can get infected, fester, and become worse.

3. Don't own someone else's anger!

Just because another person is angry and in a terrible

mood, doesn't mean you have to be. Understand it is *their* problem, not yours. Our son, Thomas, likes to say, "Nothing has meaning except the meaning I give it!"

4. Recognize the potential harm of your actions.

The use of anger may be a short-term motivator to get someone's attention for a quick behavioral change. But if it becomes your constant "tool," its effect is practically non-existent. Scripture tells us, *"By long forbearance a ruler is persuaded, and a gentle tongue breaks a bone"* (Proverbs 25:15).

5. Don't live with unresolved anger.

When your emotions trigger your temper, and is allowed to persist, it often produces long-term consequences. This is why we are told: *"In your anger do not sin; do not let the sun go down while you are still angry, and do not give the devil a foothold"* (Ephesians 4:26-27 NIV).

6. Consider the source.

Over time, I have learned to lower my expectations of certain people who demonstrate again and again that they have major "anger issues." It was their problem, and I was usually not the only person to come to that conclusion.

7. Pass what you are learning onto the next generation.

By your example, you can teach your children godly ways of dealing with their (and others') anger. Otherwise, they can grow into immature adults who behave the same way.

8. With God's help, practice self-control.

To avoid *staying* angry, I have to step back and make certain my response reflects the Fruit of the Spirit—*"...love, joy, peace, longsuffering, kindness, goodness, faithfulness, gentleness, self-control"* (Galatians 5:22-23).

This developed fruit keeps anger at bay and allows us to deal with the negative emotions of others appropriately.

Anger is connected to faith in an all-important way. It is an expression of our frustration when things don't turn out how we *expect* them to. But why were we convinced they *should* have turned out that way? Who promised us that they would?

I trust you are starting to see how faith becomes so important. People can promise us certain outcomes, but can they really control the future 100% of the time? Uncontrolled temper and rage are indeed killers of positivity, so remember: *Get rid of your unresolved anger and trust in the unfailing promises of God.*

SOMEONE IS WATCHING

Golf tournaments are much like the preliminaries of a talent show such as "The Voice," or American Idol," where the contestants are ultimately looking for a chance at a record contract. Some amateur tournaments give young players a chance to compete, hoping to win and be extended an invitation to a PGA event and make it to the next level.

At Hilton Head, South Carolina, I watched our son, Thomas, warm up for an elite amateur event, "The Players Am." There are certain guidelines and accomplishments you have to meet in order to be invited to one of these events—similar to an American Idol receiving a coveted "ticket to Hollywood."

To say the least, there was awesome talent all over that driving range. They tirelessly hit balls in the heat and were focused on the opportunity that was in front of them as they chased their dreams.

As I sat quietly, watching, something grabbed my attention. It was a small man who was happily going about his job, filling up water buckets at each spot on the range where players would clean their clubs. The sweat was pouring off him. Next, he began filling up the drinking canisters with water and ice down more cold drinks in the coolers for the players. I even saw him stop to pick up empty bottles that hadn't made it to the trash can.

Later that day while Thomas was playing, I spotted the man on the course doing the exact same thing. Still smiling. His quiet attention to his duties impressed me so much that I looked for him the next day—and, sure enough, there he was, doing his job, just as joyfully as the day before. You guessed it; the third day was more of the same.

The man had no thought of fame—being an American Idol or PGA tour player—and had no idea that someone had been watching him.

His work ethic duplicated those of the aspiring golfers: sweating, focused, and diligent. The difference to me was his "joyful" attitude.

This hard-working gentleman reminded me of Colossians 3:23-24: *"Whatever you do, work at it with all your heart, as working for the Lord, not for human masters, since you know that you will receive an inheritance from the Lord as a reward. It is the Lord Christ you are serving"* (NIV).

Perhaps we should ask ourselves, "Who are we truly trying to please? Our parents, our spouses, our coaches, our boss?" The greatest satisfaction is derived from pleasing God.

THE GIFT OF LAUGHTER

It's been quoted many times that, "Laughter is the shortest distance between two people."

The ability to find humor in life is one of the most wonderful gifts the Lord has given. I believe God knew the importance of laughter far before scientists and psychologists discovered how valuable it is to our well-being and emotional health, especially dealing with the many stresses life can bring.

We are told, *"A cheerful heart is good medicine, but a crushed spirit dries up the bones"* (Proverbs 17:22).

This verse truly applies when it comes to my sister, Marcia. She has taught me many things in life, especially about laughter, and has been "the medicine" I and others needed so many times.

I remember when we were driving home from the University Hospital in Augusta, Georgia, after taking mom there for a rather gloomy doctor's visit.

Heading home, with just the three of us in the car, things fell silent—but only for the first few minutes. Then God prompted Marcia to take us back to a childhood memory that included our mother. She proceeded to poke a little fun of the clothes mom would make for us because she really loved to sew. Actually the dresses were cute, but Marcia hammed it up, telling mom how we really wanted to wear store-bought clothes instead of those outfits she would create —which she described in hilarious detail.

For the next few minutes the three of us were laughing so hard we had to pull into a gas station for a potty break!

The Lord places certain people in our lives for special purposes.

On so many occasions, my sister has been at the right place at the right time to help make the bleakest situations bearable.

The noted writer, Hugh Sidney, made this observation: "A sense of humor...is needed armor. Joy in one's heart and some laughter on one's lips is a sign that the person down deep has a pretty good grasp of life."

As I have learned, through laughter:

1. You will worry less.
2. You will enjoy a more fulfilled life.
3. You can expose your true self (being transparent).
4. You can connect with people on a deeper level.
5. You can experience moments of significance.

Make it a habit to pay attention to those who know how to laugh; they can be some of our best teachers.

Ralph Waldo Emerson wrote these insightful words on what it means to succeed: "To laugh often and much; to win the respect of intelligent people and the affection of children; to earn the appreciation of honest critics and endure the betrayal of false friends; to appreciate beauty; to find the best in others; to leave the world a bit better, whether by a healthy child, a garden patch or a redeemed social condition; to know even one life has breathed easier because you have lived. This is to have succeeded."

HEALING THE HURTS

Everything, however, is not always peaches and cream. Life is filled with disappointments. We can all say, "could have, would have, should have," but no matter how hard we try, it is impossible to pour "spilled milk" back into the glass. So what do you do?

Our family has come to understand and live that God's Plan B is better than our Plan A! We have embraced what the Almighty said through the prophet Isaiah: *"Forget the former things; do not dwell on the past. See I am doing a new thing! Now it springs up; do you not perceive it? I am making a way in the wilderness and streams in the wasteland"* (Isaiah 43:18 NIV).

Even if your emotional wounds are still in the healing process, God is saying, *"For I know the plans I have for you...plans to prosper you and not to harm you, plans to give you hope and a future"* (Jeremiah 29:11 NIV).

Yes, the Lord has a design for each of us, but it is essential that we obey the instructions found in the next three verses: *"Then you will call on me and come and pray to me, and I will listen to you. You will seek me and find me when you seek me with all your heart. I will be found by you...and will bring you back from captivity"* (verses 12-14 NIV).

It is better to learn sooner than later that we cannot place our trust in man, or the institutions which they control. How much wiser to invest our time and energy in a relationship that links us to heaven—the source of true peace and abundance.

Of course, there will be letdowns and a few dashed hopes, but the Lord doesn't waste any experiences that come our way. He uses them to teach, redirect, mature—and often saves us from a danger we can't see.

It's not *what* happens to us, but the attitude we take, the outlook we choose, and the One in whom we place our belief and trust. We are to keep *"looking unto Jesus, the author and finisher of our faith"* (Hebrews 12:2).

Whether you have suffered a minor setback or a major loss, I encourage you to seek the Creator of your life, and allow His healing hand to mend the broken pieces and lead you beside still waters.

WHERE IS THE BALANCE?

When we hear the word "attitude," we usually think of our mental state as it relates to others, but it also includes the opinion we have of ourselves.

There is only one you! And while none of us want to be judged solely on a first look or an initial meeting (we all have bad days), we cannot discount that "first impressions" matter. How we present ourselves can open or shut doors. We only have one life and have been given one body, what the Bible calls our "temple." So it is our personal responsibility to take care of ourselves, inside and out.

Developing the attitude of always looking out for others, while putting yourself on the back burner can be a dangerous and detrimental approach. Here's the bottom line: if we neglect taking care of our personal health, we cannot take care of someone else.

Perhaps you have heard what Jesus called the second greatest command in the Bible: *"You shall love your neighbor as yourself."* And whereas this instructs us to love our neighbor, did you notice the standard by which this is to be accomplished? We love them as we love ourselves. The bottom line is simple: If we don't love ourselves properly, then we will never be able to love our neighbors as God intends.

If we let ourselves go and become run down before our time, we will eventually need to be taken care of—and to me, that's being selfish!

Maintaining balance is the key. We need to guard against going overboard in either direction.

In my late 20s, exercising became an obsession. I ran for miles, and felt guilty when I didn't clock a certain distance every week or participate in a set number of exercise classes. I was overzealous in this area.

The enemy is a master of deception—especially when you think you are doing something worthwhile.

In the Back Nine, it is essential that we pause now and again to weigh the balance in our lives. Please realize that condemnation is never from God, only conviction!

Take a long, hard look in a mirror and at your personal calendar. Learning when to say "yes" and when to say "no" is a very healthy trait. I highly recommend (and have learned the hard way) to "filter" everything through the hands of God in prayer. Giving all things to the Lord and allowing Him to direct my path has taken attention, discipline, and allotted time, and I am glad I finally adopted this lifestyle in my late

40s—something I wish I had done much earlier.

While remaining active and busy at any age is good, balance is best—in your spiritual life, appearance, emotions, and physical health. Not only will your first impression improve, so will your attitude, self-respect, and your ability to pay it forward to others.

Idols come in all shapes and sizes. They don't have to be inanimate objects, but can take the shape of seeking the praise and approval of man, saying yes to every committee and volunteer position, over-indulgence of exercise (like me in my 20s), or allowing yourself to become the dumping ground for everyone's problems.

Maybe your idol is that of being a "super mom." The mothering capsule that bursts inside of you when you have kids can be so consuming that it clouds and distorts the balance God intends for you.

Be sure to allot time in your day to take care of yourself, or you can land in a "dark hole" where it is hard to see that you are running on fumes.

UNEXPECTED ROADBLOCKS

"Oh my gosh! Oh my gosh!" I screamed those words repeatedly as I opened our kitchen door and saw water gushing from our light fixtures on a recent Sunday after church. Our ceiling in the family room was literally caving in. For the next two hours Bill and I were mopping up water along with Logan, a girl who is like a daughter to us.

It was a mess. We had an emergency team arrive within an hour to assess the problem and help us continue with the cleanup. Needless to say, the thoughts and plans I had on the drive home from church changed drastically. Allow me to explain.

We had given a party at our house on Friday for a couple who were getting married, so the house was in tip-top shape and the flowers from the celebration were beautiful. I was looking forward to an afternoon of reading, writing, and possibly cooking dinner for our neighbor who had just lost his wife a few days earlier. But my plans turned out to be different, ***very different!***

The disaster caused by the water leak was exhausting, and I went to bed thinking, "Okay, tomorrow is a brand new start."

But when I woke up the next morning, ready to seize the day, I discovered our internet was not working. Usually, I rise early, have my quiet time, then post a blog on the *Back 9* website. Instead, I was on the phone for an hour trying to get our internet service restored.

Finally, since I had to pack to head out of town, frustrated, I gave up. Nothing had been accomplished in terms of studying, writing, or posting. Then, while loading my car, I dropped the remote key and it shattered into pieces. Oh, my! As I was putting the key back together, I began asking God to intervene and help—to encourage and protect me. I realized that all the stops and roadblocks that had happened in the last 24 hours were "spiritual warfare."

You may not see it this way and that's okay...but I do. Satan is the prince of the world and until Christ returns he is alive and well, seeking to divert, discourage, and even destroy those who love Jesus and are actively seeking Him.

In the past few years, since I have taken up writing, strange and unexplainable things have gone haywire with my emails, my computer blacking out, keys freezing, etc. Almost every time these breakdowns occurred while I was in the midst of working on Back 9 ministry details. We should never forget what Scripture tells us in Ephesians 6:10-13: *"Finally, be strong in the Lord and in his mighty power. Put on the full armor of God, so that you can take your stand against the devil's schemes. For our struggle is not against flesh and blood, but against the rulers, against the authorities, against the powers of this dark world and against the spiritual forces of evil in the heavenly realms. Therefore put on the full armor of God, so that when the day of evil comes, you may be able to stand your ground, and after you have done everything, to stand"* (NIV).

I also believe it was not a coincidence that the day before the emergency at our home, I spoke to a group of young woman on the topic of purity and the importance of leading a godly life in Christ.

I've learned not to be surprised or dismayed, but to lean heavily on the Lord, asking Him to clear the path, to free the "dam of roadblocks," and give me peace in the process.

The Lord has not only been faithful, but I've had a chance to meet wonderful workmen—including those from the Rainbow emergency team, the sheet rock installers, and even the AT&T internet technician.

Today, let me encourage you to march forward. Never allow Satan to get you so focused on the "fallen tree" lying in your path that you fail to see the "baby birds in the nest" you otherwise would not have noticed if the tree had not fallen.

God can—and will—take the most frustrating circumstances and use them for His glory.

Look for the positive in the negative. The Lord will give you special "sight" to see His hand at work.

As Corrie Ten Boom once said, "The first step on the way to victory is to recognize the enemy."

YOU ARE NOT ALONE

Having unshakeable faith, getting rid of anger, laughing more, healing the hurts, and loving yourself properly can seem like a lot to do to eventually become a positive person, but remember that you are not alone.

If willpower and determination are required, rely on the fact that God is your source: *"'Not by might nor by power, but by My spirit,' says the Lord of hosts"* (Zechariah 4:6).

Making a course correction begins with a change of attitude. Instead of trying to do everything on your own, hear Jesus say, *"Without Me you can do nothing"* (John 15:5).

You have amazing help!

NOTES FOR YOUR SCORECARD

- Negativity is a disease that not only affects us personally, but is contagious.
- Being confident and optimistic requires faith, trust, intention, discipline, and constant self-examination.
- Determine that you will not live another day with unresolved anger.
- Laughter is God's medicine for our emotional health.
- It's not what happens to us, but how we choose to respond.
- If we fail to take care of ourselves, how can we take care of others?
- A change of direction begins with a change of attitude.

TEE #12
OBJECTIVES

Those who say they don't have any problems are either missing or ignoring reality. I rarely buy into the canned remarks that everything is "good," "great," or "wonderful."

When a person constantly gives only glowing responses, they are either being considerate, prideful, or suppressing the truth. We often see this played out on our Facebook profiles, pictures, and statuses.

Personally, in the first half of my life, I dealt with hundreds of problems—some of which I have shared only with God. I have also come to realize that certain issues take a very long time to solve and a few, in the natural, seem impossible. I have also discovered that if I do my best, with the right motives—even though there are still painful emotions—and if I go through the process of addressing the steps involved in problem solving—things get a whole lot better. This is true even if the solution doesn't immediately come to light.

The skills I have embraced, and want to share with you, make a very important assumption about the person applying them, namely that you value your relationships. They (along with your emotions and your character) play a significant role in how you go about solving problems. It is more than just logic and good common sense; there is context and mind, body, and soul to take into account.

In this chapter, we will zero in on the role your feelings

and emotions play in personal achievement. In the process, you will learn how to choose wise counsel, connect with others, and the importance of visualizing your objectives. Plus, we will discuss sure-fire solutions in dealing with problems.

God is no stranger to our difficulties and certainly holds the wisdom to help us untangle any situation. The Lord gave us tools, including a computer-like brain, to use in effectively dealing with and addressing any circumstance. This is a game-changer!

Let's flesh out these steps/tools together.

SOLVING PROBLEMS AND REACHING OBJECTIVES INVOLVES EMOTIONS

The first step in problem solving is to look at the emotions that bubble up when a troubling issue arises.

Most challenges are negative, so the emotions surrounding them usually fall into the same category—fear, frustration, sadness, anger, just to name a few. Our emotions are God-given. They are our alert signals that we are neither to deny or let rule. We are to recognize and label them based on what we are feeling, and use them to drive us to solutions. They shouldn't control our every whim.

Albert Einstein observed, "Feeling and longing are the motive forces behind all human endeavor and human creations." And Psalm 139:23 indicates we are prone to worry: *"Search me, O God, and know my heart; try me, and know my anxieties."*

Your feelings can be used as your servants to reveal and help identify problems. They can cause you to pay attention to troubles, but emotions are never intended to be your master. Over time, if you tell yourself not to feel a certain way, or to stop for fear of falling into self-pity, you are not letting your natural emotions become the trigger that causes you to look at a difficulty that needs to be solved. You are denying the feelings instead of verbalizing to yourself, "You are darn right I am angry. I am hurt and feel terrible!"

The next question is, "Okay God. What do You want me to do with my emotions?"

For example, when we are angry, people may advise us to stop and count to ten before we react.

Our outburst is sometimes justified, but our actions may not be if we lash out in retaliation.

Anger, when it is acknowledged, labeled, and examined within ourselves, can be used to identify the source of our frustration. Only then can we logically take the next step.

Perhaps you have heard the saying, "Hurting people hurt people." This is true—and another example of raw emotions. The truth is that hurting people don't stop to recognize their own feelings and trace the source. They are often *unaware* of how their "suppressed hurt" manifests itself by inflicting pain on others. Denial of their own emotions has blinded them to their heartache and, in turn, they have no idea they are causing anguish to someone else.

In any situation, the only thing you can do is *what you can do.* You are responsible for recognizing and examining your feelings and dealing with them accordingly.

God created us with a myriad of emotions for many reasons. When paid attention to, they give us valuable insight. Denying your feelings and stifling them depletes the energy you need to embrace, label, and address the root cause. When painful issues are not faced and dealt with, they get suppressed—and can then manifest as other obstacles. The effort it takes to crush painful emotions when they surface can be draining mentally and physically.

Your objective is to work through the situation and put it in the rear view mirror!

Learning to recognize and label your feelings is a healthy approach to life. It puts you one step closer to the "clear head" needed to address a predicament without piling new problems on top of old ones. Now you are able to start uncovering how to solve the problem that caused the emotions to reveal themselves.

"Old school" thinking makes fun of getting in touch with your inner-self. I disagree one hundred percent with this approach. Learn to use emotions as your servants. Identify and acknowledge them and let them be the spark of hope that takes you to the next step—which is to get with the right people. As King Solomon wrote, *"Counsel in the heart of man is like deep water, but a man of understanding will draw it out"* (Proverbs 20:5).

SOLVING PROBLEMS AND REACHING OBJECTIVES REQUIRES RELATIONSHIPS

I came across a quotation by the first century Roman philosopher, Seneca, that could have been written today: "Consult your friend on all things, especially on those which respect yourself. His counsel may then be useful where your own self-love might impair your judgement."

When a big and painful problem presents itself in marriage, finances, or family relationships, a major human tendency is to withdraw. We pull our head into a shell like a turtle, or hibernate in a "cave" or just allow our thoughts to circle or run off cliffs.

Spending time alone and praying in order to deal with and shine a spotlight on our emotions is not a bad thing but remaining isolated can be extremely harmful! On the other hand, relationships with the "right people" can be *crucial* in solving problems.

I love the passage found in Ecclesiastes 4:9-12: *"Two are better than one, because they have a good reward for their labor. For if they fall, one will lift up his companion. But woe to him who is alone when he falls, for he has no one to help him up. Again, if two lie down together, they will keep warm; But how can one be warm alone? Though one may be overpowered by another, two can withstand him. And a threefold cord is not quickly broken."*

We were created for relationship; it is God's design. Having a connection with people who know us well and who we trust enough to allow them on the "inside" can be a life bridge when problems occur—and they will.

It is also vital to remember that these relationships are key when we celebrate the "winning times."

Keeping to ourselves and trying to "go it alone" is not a virtue, it is a weakness— a sign of pride and self-sufficiency!

Regardless of your track record on reaching out to others for help, it is never too late to start.

CONNECTION AND REALITY

There are two important elements involving relationships in the midst of struggles: connection and reality! Connection provides fuel for life—a blanket of love, comfort, support, empathy, and encouragement. As the scripture above tells us, someone to walk beside you and "keep you warm."

It is a well-documented fact that those who allow "safe people" into their lives during storms have a higher quality of life and are better prepared to solve what they are facing.

We can all get caught in the trap of thinking our situation is one of a kind and no one else on the planet has ever come against what we are encountering. But the truth of the matter is that there is only a finite number of problems in the world. Chances are you know a friend or can find an individual who can help you "navigate" the same waters they have safely crossed before you! This is connection—finding commonalities with men and women who help us weather the storms of life. And we can, in turn, do the same for others. Dr. John Townsend uses the analogy of "snowflakes." Even though all are unique and different, they can all be used to make a "snowman!" I love that!

THE REALITY FACTOR

How does reality fit into relationships?

It means evaluating what is happening at the moment and figuring out what to do about the difficulty today. We need folks who can help steer us on the rivers of life, those with whom we connect right now.

When circumstances are overwhelming, turn to a person

of character and trust who has demonstrated a good track record in decision-making. Find an individual who cares for you enough to speak "truth in love." You will gain perspective, *sound* discernment and guidance. What a blessing to know you are not alone.

A prime example in Scripture that gives us a visual of having the right relationships during difficult days is found in Exodus 17:10-12: *"So Joshua did as Moses said to him, and fought with Amalek. And Moses, Aaron, and Hur went up to the top of the hill. And so it was, when Moses held up his hand, that Israel prevailed; and when he let down his hand, Amalek prevailed. But Moses' hands became heavy; so they took a stone and put it under him, and he sat on it. And Aaron and Hur supported his hands, one on one side, and the other on the other side; and his hands were steady until the going down of the sun."*

The Israelites were winning as long as Moses held his staff in the air. When he became weary of the reality before him, Aaron and Hur were by his side—to steady him until the battle was over.

Never be too afraid or too proud to enlist the help of godly, quality friends. These are the relationships that provide the strength and support the Bible talks about when we are facing a trial.

I have heard it said, "No road is long with the right company!"

A word of caution: If you are like me, you want to be very careful to not lean on friends too much or run to them with every detail of your life. Pray for wisdom. I have learned to make sure I have more than one friend with the same qualities. When I do call, I want to be sensitive to where they are on their life's journey and not infringe on their privacy. If they are in the midst of a personal dilemma or busy with their own family, I try to schedule an appropriate time to talk.

Some pot holes are quick fixes, but there are instances that require a friend to invest considerable time walking beside you. During one major challenge, thankfully, I had several friends who helped guide me through. It allowed us to manage our time and other commitments. It also gave me the advantage of learning from several perspectives and experiences.

God has people waiting in the wings to throw life preservers your way! Seek them out. Let them walk with you through the reality of a setback.

SOLVING PROBLEMS AND REACHING OBJECTIVES REQUIRES CLARITY

When I ask my family the simple question, "What would you like for dinner?" The answer is often, "Oh, not chicken. But it really doesn't matter!"

Their response is really not helpful to me. I am looking for some clarity but all I get is vague or mixed messages! Or, if I am planning a special occasion and ask, "Where would you like to go?" and the answer is, "Oh, it doesn't matter. You pick!"—I can become so frustrated. I have to stop myself from responding, "Duh! If I wanted to pick, I wouldn't have asked you!"

Clarity is a good thing. Since God is a God of order, He does not desire for anyone to live in a state of confusion, becoming lost in an uncertain "grey area."

When a problem invades our territory, our tendency is to obsess, camp out, pick apart, over-analyze, or whine about it far too long. Defining where a difficulty originates and where it ends can be very helpful. Also, rating the degree of the issue as mild, moderate or severe provides vital information. For example:

- **Mild:** Someone notices a "tire" around your mid-section and suggests you need to lose a couple of pounds. Or, you're having a "bad hair" day.
- **Moderate:** Your child came home with a bad mid-term grade. You didn't receive that counted-on bonus. You failed to make the baseball team or cheerleading squad, etc.
- **Severe:** Marriage issues, illness, child on drugs, death, etc.

It is human nature to allow troubles to magnify, multiply, and even take over our lives, redefining every healthy area. This is why simple steps of transparency and definition are essential in working toward solving problems and reaching objectives.

First, take the time to find a quiet place to think through your quandary in terms of measurement and to gain perspective: *"Be still, and know that I am God..."* (Psalm 46:10).

The Lord can bring peace in literal storms. Once when a great tempest appeared on the Sea of Galilee, Jesus *"arose and rebuked the wind, and said to the seas, 'Peace, be still!' And the wind ceased and there was a great calm"* (Mark 4:39). What a reassurance that God can bring His perfect peace.

Certainly when a problem is "severe," there may be a season of intense focus needed—and it can redefine your life for a period of time. Type 1 Diabetes did that for me, our son Thomas, and our entire family. But, thank goodness, I knew enough about the process in solving or addressing "messes" and misfortunes that I was able to find a calm assurance in the midst of our storm.

Utilizing the principles outlined in this chapter, brought order, focus, clarity, peace, and direction. It didn't take away the pain or sadness, but it *moved* me and united our family toward a solution.

Placing parameters on a problem lets you know where it starts and where it ends. For me, I had two other children, a husband, and a busy household to run. A "chronic illness" was certainly serious, but it could not dominate every aspect of our lives. Yes, it changed how we did certain things, but we all had to adapt.

With God's help, we defined diabetes;
we did not let it define us!

So be careful. Never allow problems to derail everything else that matters to you!

Establishing boundaries also brings patience and diligence. It puts you into the "Git-Er-Done" mode!

We must understand the definition of delayed gratification. If I faithfully do the right thing every day, even though I don't see the results immediately, I trust they will follow.

Decide on these objectives:

- I will love people.
- I will reconnect.
- I will take action.
- I will take responsibility.
- I will admit when I make a mistake.

By doing these things, I will find comfort and peace in knowing that, in time, I will reap a harvest!

As an adult I have come to absolutely know that I cannot respond like a child who stomps his or her feet demanding "My way now!" Some problems will not be resolved in my time frame. Grasping the sowing and reaping principle, daily putting in the investment to solve dilemmas, and not demanding drive-thru gratification have been areas the Lord has redefined in the last decade of my life!

Learning to establish order and clarity in dealing with certain predicaments produces patience, peace, and progress! As the psalmist wrote, *"In peace I will both lie down and sleep; for you alone, O Lord, make me dwell in safety"* (Psalm 4:8).

A New Perspective

In the Back Nine of life, God smiles at me daily and perhaps even chuckles! I know He does because He can read my mind and knows my thoughts! So He may be the only one smiling—and it is between the two of us. But I find a great comfort and intimacy, especially when I know the Lord is saying, "Out of the mouths of babes!"—and then laughs!

I had such a moment when our oldest, Brewer, came home for a visit. We sometimes call him "Brew-Daddy," especially when profound things flow out of his mouth.

We were relaxing, sitting by the fire and, after giving me just a few minutes of his ear on the topic of exercise, he simply said to me, "Mom, that is not a real problem. You are over 50. You don't have to run marathons like me to keep in shape!"

He was spot on! I was muddying the waters in my mind over something that really didn't exist. Such fabricated worries usually center on a reality that is not changing—such as age, the death of a loved one, a chronic illness, or the ending of a relationship. Incorporating someone, even a mature young adult, to be the gauge on reality can be extremely helpful.

A second pair of eyes can help determine if there is a real problem that needs to be accepted and adjusted to, with an appropriate and needed response.

Certainly we need to give the matter time, but then we must move on. Those who experience the death of a loved one often, in their grief and loss, struggle to find God's peace and rest which could enable them to continue life in a new normal. I am not an authority on this by any means, but I have witnessed friends who, by God's grace, have taken the appropriate steps in terrible circumstances and found the miraculous (while not instantaneous) road to recovery and life!

Job faced unbearable obstacles. Hear him cry, *"For the thing that I greatly feared has come upon me, and what I dreaded has happened to me. I am not at ease, nor am I quiet; I have no rest, for trouble comes"* (Job 3:25-26). But we find the answer in Psalm 29:11: *"The Lord will give strength to His people; the Lord will bless His people with peace!"*

When Brew-Daddy pointed out that I was not 25 and, in reality, was probably not going to run marathons again, I needed to accept, embrace it, and simply move on.

I smiled, God smiled, and that was that!

It really wasn't a problem, just an adjustment to reality! Can't stop that thing called age!

What if it had remained a downer in my mind and spiraled out of control? That kind of thinking can lead to "insanity!" Moving to a different "happy place" is a much better option.

The question to ask is, "What is my objective? If this problem gets solved, what do I want the end result to be?" This pushes you into a positive mindset.

When I run to God with my troubles, that's where I can clearly see His hand of guidance. He is there waiting, not always with a quick fix, but is preparing the steps and the answer.

I love what noted Christian psychologist John Townsend says concerning this: "If you only think about the problem and never about your desires, you are constantly playing defense in life, not offense!" He also states, "Life isn't fundamentally about solving problems. Life is about God, relationships, and purpose. Solving problems gets the speed bumps out of the way so that you can live the life God wants for you!"

To that I say, "Amen!"

NOTES FOR YOUR SCORECARD

- Your emotions play a key role in solving problems and reaching objectives.
- Pay attention to your feelings; they give you valuable insights.
- Instead of withdrawing, seek the counsel of godly friends.
- Your connection to others provides fuel for life.
- Face reality by finding someone who will speak truth in love.
- Seek clarity and definition before taking action.
- Visualizing your objective gives you a positive mindset.
- Never allow problems to derail all the other positives in your life.
- Isolate your problem, if at all possible.
- Drive-thru gratification in solving some issues doesn't exist—it requires patience, perseverance, and time.

Tee #13
Commitment

It was Thursday on a hot summer day in Westminster, South Carolina. Mom and I were at the Winn-Dixie grocery store to do the weekly shopping. I was just six years old but remember it well.

Mom always made sure she chose the checkout lane of her friend, a tall, thin blonde named "Flo."

As we were standing in line, waiting, I saw this big, clear jar of Bazooka bubble gum, with each piece wrapped in red, white, and blue paper. It only cost one cent each, but I didn't have a penny. I knew if I asked for gum, the answer would be no! So, when no one was looking, I reached in the jar and sneaked a piece. And as we walked to the car, I popped it in my mouth.

On the way home, my mother noticed that I was chewing gum and asked me, "Where did you get that?"

Guilt, fear, and tears set in all at once. To this day I can remember what I was wearing: red shorts and a white top. I really don't have very many memories of being six, except for walking back into that grocery store to confess to Flo what I had done—and giving her a penny for the gum. I was utterly mortified as I faced the situation of my own making!

This was the first and only time I can ever remember stealing, and can honestly say I have never taken anything since that wasn't mine. It was an extremely painful but very valuable lesson on how my parents felt about shoplifting.

In the hectic fray of today's world, I hope and pray that all parents would make a big deal of such an incident. If the kids are older than six, especially in their middle years, there should be far more serious consequences. Stealing is wrong on all levels, and a commitment to honesty is an issue of character and heart.

The issue of honesty is just one aspect of what we will address in this chapter. I want you to understand the necessity of instilling integrity and character in the lives of those you influence. Establishing values, possessing a "moral code," and making a commitment to strengthen your "earthly temple" are vital to fulfilling the purpose God has planned for you.

WHO IS THE TEACHER?

Bill and I have been fortunate to know and be friends of Eric Hyman and his beautiful wife, Pauline, for a number of years. Our friendship began while he was the Athletic Director at the University of South Carolina, before he moved on to Texas A&M. I truly learned so much from them—up close and at a distance.

I remember Eric being quoted in the *State* newspaper, referring to college students, especially athletes, and he said, "They come to college with integrity. They don't find it when they get here!"

I absolutely agree.

Integrity and character are meant to be established by

parents. We should teach and model values, then hold our children to a standard with a very high bar. Of course, as parents we can't catch everything our kids do, but if we are involved and choose to be active and engaged moms and dads, willing to take the time and the patience to be role models to our sons and daughters, we can observe and teach many valuable lessons.

As parents, we have a huge responsibility to our children. We owe them our wisdom and experience, and they should be taught the majority of this at home.

It would be marvelous if all mature adults reinforced these principles, but unfortunately, that is not always the case.

I have learned to lower my expectations of some individuals who interact with our kids. I use those encounters as teachable moments to talk to our children about character, especially if it involves adults in leadership or authority over them. Some of those "in charge" just plain and simply do not live according to the highest of standards.

The dictionary defines integrity as *honesty*—adherence to moral and ethical principles; soundness of moral character. We either have it or we don't.

A Commitment that Pays Lifetime Benefits

Allow me to share seven benefits of living, examining, "shoring up," and teaching integrity:

First: Living with integrity brings wholeness and peace.

Your conscience (some have had their conscience seared—Romans 1:28-32 and 1 Timothy 4:1-2) can rest easy and you can sleep soundly at night knowing you did the right thing, regardless of the outcome.

Second: You are trusted by others.

A person with integrity can be counted on and respected. All their relationships will be healthier, stronger and more satisfying.

Third: A commitment to integrity allows one clarity when they have to make hard choices.

You will not be at "war with yourself" over the path you should choose. It will be clear and will breed confidence. You will avoid living in the realm of constantly being tossed about like a ball on the waves of an ocean, changing your mind or your word according to the circumstances.

Fourth: Having a value system, "a moral code," that you are committed to not compromise is valuable for a lifetime.

Establishing this allows one to build a reputation of trust and respect that grows with time. These virtues have to be earned. Regardless of how you have lived in the past, if trust is lost, so is respect. It has been said, "It takes years to earn a good reputation, and a day or one decision to lose it!"

Fifth: There will always be one million reasons to rationalize and compromise a value system and moral code.

Excuses may seem to make good sense at the time and

may help you sleep at night after an ill-gotten victory, but over time, the lack of a moral code can lead to devastation.

One small justification leads to another (it blackens your conscience and self-denial sets in). Before long, the slope is slippery and you are gliding downhill. Time catches up, and when it does, you find yourself scratching your head asking, "How did I get here?"

A very public example is bicycle racing legend Lance Armstrong. He attained worldwide acclaim and success, wrote books, traveled the globe, and spoke to millions, but his small decisions, left unchecked, led to total and utter devastation on the large media stage.

You don't have to be famous like Lance to lose complete respect and trust from those you live around and with whom you interact.

If you love or have a relationship with someone, you will gently call them out in an area where they are slipping in integrity. It really isn't up to you if they listen. Of more importance is that you cared enough to do the hard but right thing by confronting them—Scripture calls it "speak the truth in love."

Some who live with a deficiency of character may be able to get away with it for a lifetime. However, I have a difficult time wrapping my mind around them truly enjoying personal peace and satisfaction unless their conscience has been greatly seared. Unfortunately, such people exist in all walks of life.

Sixth: A person's lack of integrity (honesty) doesn't just suddenly happen.

A collapse of character takes place one small decision or

compromise at a time, followed by rationalization and justification. It is a dangerous, life-destroying way to live.

Seventh: We must constantly monitor our daily decisions and words to make sure they line up with an honest moral code.

True success is the result of godly principles. There are tons of scriptures on the topic:

- *"He who walks with integrity walks securely, but he who perverts his ways will become known"* (Proverbs 10:9).
- *"The integrity of the upright will guide them, but the perversity of the unfaithful will destroy them"* (Proverbs 11:3).
- *"For the Lord gives wisdom; from His mouth come knowledge and understanding; He stores up sound wisdom for the upright; He is a shield to those who walk uprightly; He guards the paths of justice, and preserves the way of His saints"* (Proverbs 2:6-8).

God intends for all mankind to walk and live with personal integrity: it leads to a significant and satisfying life.

SUNDAY GOLF

Over the past few years, Sundays (for the most part), have been spent on the golf course. This became a soul-searching struggle for me, having been raised to go to church on

Sunday morning, as well as Sunday night.

Finding myself with three children playing competitive golf year round lent itself to having to worship differently than most. It was uncharted territory.

After a few years of missing church because of the weekend tournaments, I felt like the withered plant that sits on my back porch. I had good intentions to worship, but it just wasn't working out. The nudging voice inside me, the Holy Spirit, was affording me no rest or peace on this matter.

I began inquiring how other people involved in golf handled the issue. I started with the Christians on the PGA tour—Webb Simpson, Ben Crane, Stewart Cink, Jonathan Byrd, Aaron Badley, and Payne Stewart—just to name a few. I found they had early morning, *very* early morning, services on Sundays when on tour and that most of them treated Monday as their Sunday, a day of rest. In junior golf, however, the only early church service that was ever provided was on Easter Sunday.

More than once I have heard people comment, "You don't have to go to church to worship and really know God." But I just couldn't buy into that line of thinking. To me, a Bible-believing and teaching church is a representation of Christ, and growing up in church did more for me than just about anything else I have ever done in my life. Week after week I was taught who Jesus was by people who had studied and known the Lord longer than I had.

- Attending church taught me about Jesus. I learned that if you don't know God's Word, you can't possibly know His will.

- Attending church gave me exceptional role models and lifelong friends.
- Attending church put people in my path who genuinely cared about my spiritual growth and held me accountable.
- Attending church gave me great fellowship.
- Attending church provided a refuge and support when adversity hit.
- Attending church challenged me to become a better person, and the church loved me countless times when I wasn't very lovable.

At one time or another, we are all guilty of being hypocrites. So to say the church is full of them, I agree. I belong in this category because I am a sinner, but a sinner seeking to be sin-less. With that being said, you can see how I desperately needed to find a way to have church weekly, and I preferred to have it on Sunday.

WHAT WAS THE ANSWER?

After much prayer and asking God, "Please help me and show me the way!" He did. I discovered that great Christian ministers and churches provided online podcasts so that I could have an early morning worship wherever I found myself on Sunday. (After several years, my own home church started posting podcasts too!)

I immediately bought a laptop and started enjoying worship again on Sunday mornings. It was like being dehydrated and having a bag of B12 and IV fluids running through my veins.

As I continued to pray for guidance, the Lord graciously revealed to me that I could take what I was learning to the golf course in the form of evangelism. I could actually *live* what I was hoping my children would do: be Christ to others. What this came to mean was an opportunity to share my faith and my struggles with other parents who were also following their children on the golf circuit. After all, any round of golf takes at least four hours, which allowed plenty of time, if an open door presented itself, to get to know someone. I would try to find common ground to share with parents and loved ones as we followed our kids during their round. I would see many of these people multiple times, and over the years several became dear friends. Watching our children play golf took on a whole new meaning to me.

I would like to say that I took advantage of every opportunity 100% of the time, but I didn't. Sometimes either the timing wasn't right or people weren't open or receptive. There were days when my heart wasn't right and times I was just led to pray alone.

God is forever faithful to answer our prayers. He more than showed me how to live Romans 12:1-2 on the golf course: *"I urge you, brothers and sisters, in view of God's mercy, to offer your bodies as a living sacrifice, holy and pleasing to God—this is your true and proper worship. Do not conform to the pattern of this world, but be transformed by the renewing of your mind. Then you will be able to test and approve what God's will is—his good, pleasing and perfect will"* (NIV).

And I had a new appreciation for James 4:8: *"Draw near*

to God, and He will draw near to you."

DANIEL'S DIET

My commitment to the Lord, has involved much more than finding time to worship when I am on the road. It extends to many other aspects of life.

For example, if you asked any of my lunch or dinner buddies what I liked to eat, they'd tell you, "Fried chicken, mashed potatoes, or a cheeseburger, French fries, and a Diet Coke."

During the Front Nine of my life, those were my meals of choice and friends didn't mind telling me those were triple bogies for sure!

Well, passing the half-century mark, I decided to *change my ways.* It's amazing how long it takes for God to get your attention in certain areas of your life. It took turning 50 and, yes, feeling it at times! I knew I had terrible eating habits, so I was using AdvoCare nutritional products to offset my bad food choices and fill in the gaps with nutrition that I wasn't getting from the food I was consuming. But as I began reading the book of Daniel, God so convicted my heart that I made a commitment for even more substantial changes.

For Bible readers, this will be a very familiar story. But perhaps you are like me and need to hear it again.

In Daniel chapter 1, we find there was a king of Babylon named Nebuchadnezzar, who conquered another leader, Jehoiakim, King of Judah, and his people. Nebuchadnezzar decided to take into his palace some of the young men from Judah and place them in a three-year training program, learning to serve in the kingdom.

Four men in particular were chosen for this golden opportunity: Daniel and his three friends, Shadrach, Meshach, and Abednego. They were being groomed with many others and were asked to eat the royal diet, which was filled with rich food and wine.

Daniel went to the chief of the eunuchs and asked if they could deviate from the "menu" and eat fruits, vegetables, and drink water. The chief's response was, "I am afraid of my lord the king, who has assigned your food and drink. If he saw you looking worse than the other young men your age, the king would then have my head!"

However, the chief took a huge risk and allowed Daniel his request for ten days, after which a comparison was made of all the men. The "fruit, vegetable, and water men" looked healthier and better nourished than any of the young trainees who ate the king's fare. So the steward assigned them to do away with the rich food and go with Daniel's diet.

At the end of the three years, Nebuchadnezzar found "none equal" to Daniel, and his three friends. In fact, they were ten times better than all the magicians and enchanters in his whole kingdom.

Well, this story hit home! Finally, on the Back Nine of life, I have greatly improved my eating habits. Unfortunately, I had set a terrible example for our kids in this area, but as they grew older, they figured it out without their mother's help.

The Bible has countless lessons on how we should treat

our bodies, which God calls our "earthly temple." This is why I made a commitment to pay much closer attention to what I eat, realizing that our lives become a sum total of our choices.

A COMMITMENT TO LEADERSHIP

On September 8, 2014, when I heard that Truett Cathy had passed away, it brought back a rush of memories.

If ever there was a man who personified the word "commitment," it was Truett, the founder of the fast-food giant, Chick-fil-A.

Here was a person who was sold out to Christ and walked the talk all of his life. He taught Sunday school to young boys for 50 years.

Starting with one small store in Hapville, Georgia, in 1946, he built his sprawling restaurant empire on hard work, humility and biblical principles—which included a commitment to close all Chick-fil-A's on Sunday, "without exception." This was to honor his personal convictions of having a day of rest, even if it meant lost sales.

Truett was a dedicated husband, father, grandfather and great-grandfather. His two sons, Dan and Don ("Bubba"), have both followed their father in learning the business from the ground up. Dan became president and chief operating officer of Chick-fil-A in 2001. Bubba is senior vice president and heads the WinShape Foundation, shaping winners by offering scholarships establishing youth programs that are faith-based and teach leadership principles.

Cathy's daughter, Trudy (White) serves as the director of the WinShape Girls Camps.

I fondly remember hearing Truett's son, Dan, speak at a college graduation several years ago where my dad and uncle were being presented with an "honorary doctorate degree" from Anderson University—the only degree my dad and his identical twin brother, Sam, have ever received. I was deeply impressed with the content of Dan's speech, and his personal commitment to continue the legacy of his father.

Truett made this profound statement, by which he lived his life: "Nearly every moment of every day we have the opportunity to give something to someone else, our time, our love, our resources. I have always found more joy in giving when I did not expect anything in return."

This is a marvelous example of true leadership—one that I have seen firsthand in my father and his twin!

DOUBLE YOUR TALENT

I believe when we pass from this life and go to our great reward, the Lord will be eagerly awaiting to say these words that we find in Matthew 25:23: *"Well done, good and faithful servant! you have been faithful over a few things; I will put you in charge of many things. Come and share your master's happiness!"* (NIV).

In this "Parable of the Talents," Jesus tells the story of a man, better known as a Master, who had talents (a form of money) which he entrusted to his servants to use and develop into more talents. In the parable, we see Jesus as the Master and ourselves in the role of the servants. The man gave five talents to one servant, two to another, and one to another according to their abilities. Then the landowner left for a journey.

The journey is symbolic of Christ dying on the cross, going to heaven and sending the Holy Spirit to be with us. Giving us a choice to receive Jesus to be the Master of our life, thus allowing the Spirit to enable us to do great things that Jesus purposed in advance for you and me to do with our talents and abilities!

The Lord goes on to tell the "choices" each of the servants made. On the master's return, one servant exclaimed, "Look, I took the five talents and doubled them. Here are five more."

That's when the master congratulated him for being a good and faithful servant and said that he would be put in charge of many things.

The servant who was entrusted with two talents and also doubled them, was given the same promise. But the man who had been allotted just one talent said to the landowner, *"Lord, I knew you to be a hard man, reaping where you have not sown, and gathering where you have not scattered seed. And I was afraid, and went and hid your talent in the ground. Look, there you have what is yours"* (verses 24-25).

His master replied, *"You wicked, lazy servant, you knew that I reap where I have not sown, and gather where I have not scattered seed, So you ought to have deposited my money with the bankers, and at my coming I would have received back my own with interest"* (verses 26-27).

He goes on to say, *"Therefore take the talent from him and give it to him who has ten talents. For to everyone who has, more will be given, and he will have abundance; but from him who does not have, even what he has will be taken away. And cast the unprofitable servant into the outer darkness. There will be weeping and gnashing of teeth"* (verses 28-30).

I love how Jesus uses money as a major illustration of instruction. My dad always taught me, "When you deal with people and it involves money, you will learn all you ever want to know about that person."

Now that I am on the Back Nine of life, I understand at a much deeper level what my father meant. How you manage finances reveals your personal commitment and character.

To me, a more profound meaning of the parable is how we spend our life on this earth and handle the talents (both monetary and non-monetary) that have been entrusted to us. While it is true that God may give more to some than others, we each have been blessed with at least *one* talent. The Lord's expectation is *maximization!* At the very least we should make a commitment to double, what has been placed into our lives.

Thinking about this story inspires me to multiply my efforts. At this age, I might move a tad slower, but retire? Not a chance. I have yet to find that word in the Bible!

God's desire is for His children to share in His glory and His happiness. He longs to give us more, but we have to double or triple our gifts and abilities—not worrying how or when He chooses to scatter seed or when He decides to bring in the harvest.

The Lord has provided His Word, Himself, and the Holy Spirit. He made the ultimate commitment to us, and now it's our turn.

NOTES FOR YOUR SCORECARD

- Parents must make a commitment to instill integrity and character into the lives of their children.
- Integrity brings peace, trust, clarity, and establishes a "moral code."
- We must never compromise our value system.
- Make a commitment to constantly monitor your words and actions.
- You can always find a time and a place for worship.
- Make a commitment to strengthen your "earthly temple."
- The talents you have been given are not to be buried, but multiplied.

TEE #14
ENCOURAGEMENT

I can remember like it was yesterday—being crowned Miss South Carolina!

At the moment of the announcement it seemed so surreal. The lights flashing, people clapping, and the music playing. As I walked and waved, I had inner thoughts of, "Wow! I can hardly believe it happened. I actually won!"

There was a flurry of emotion, relief, excitement, and adrenaline all surging at one time. It seemed like forever before the "realness" set in.

After the hugs and congratulations from all the contestants, I finally got to see my parents, sister, and my extended family. It was so good to put my arms around their necks and celebrate an accomplishment in which they not only supported me, but had gone over and above in every way to provide the best opportunity for me to succeed. My sister, Marcia, has always been my biggest cheerleader!

However, there is a moment that stands out as vividly as hearing my name called. It is when my dad took the opportunity to take me aside for a private moment to say some very meaningful words.

As the years have flown by, I have come to recognize just how wise those words were, for many reasons.

Dad said, "Sherry, we all couldn't be more proud of you! I love you and you have worked hard and are very deserving.

We all praise God for allowing you this accomplishment, but I would like to remind you of a few things."

I thought, "Oh, what could this possibly be about."

He began, "First, every girl on this stage probably worked equally as hard, and is now very disappointed. Don't forget that. And second, understand, you won based on six people's opinion. It is not the whole world's opinion, so with that being said, a different week and six different judges, there may have been another winner."

At first, I was a little taken back: "What?" Then I realized, he just wanted me to stay grounded.

I had a crown on my head, but he really did not want it to change me, his daughter!

I got the message. He was being a wise father by living out Proverbs 25:1, which states, *"A word fitly spoken is like apples of gold in settings of silver."* My dad realized that, with success, the danger of pride can set in very quickly.

This is just one of the life-lessons I learned and have never forgotten. So on this "tee" I want to share the importance of speaking truth in love by helping, not hurting, how to be sensitive to the feelings of others, and how personal growth requires accountability. We'll also discuss the fine art of empathizing with a friend who may be wounded and suffering.

Funny how two months later, standing on the stage in Atlantic City at the Miss America pageant, I was absorbing the loss of being so close to winning, to the point of a tie, and coming up short.

Once again, Dad pulled me to the side. He said almost

the exact same words, "Sherry, we could not be more proud of you. I know that you are disappointed. You have worked extremely hard and have represented our family so well but, more importantly, our state. I know you did not win, but you are still our winner. Please don't forget, a different week and a different group of judges, you may have been Miss America. It is not the world's opinion. It is just six people. God has a plan."

You cannot believe how his sage advice took away so much of the sting of losing. The words of my father were comforting and healing—almost immediately.

THE DANGERS OF SUCCESS

I have been able to take those wise words, so "fitly spoken," and use them with our own children. Even though none of them have competed in pageants, there were times when they have been picked over to play for their golf teams. I've been able to encourage them by pointing out, "It's just the opinion of one person, not the world."

My father never competed in sports and certainly not pageants, but oh the wisdom. He was proud of me but recognized the dangers of success and how certain factors can creep in and take hold. I am so grateful for the times my parents and my Uncle Sam and Aunt Joellen spoke godly counsel into my life.

Let me encourage you—people of all ages and stages—to read God's Word. Absorb what it teaches because it is an instruction manual for life, especially the book of Proverbs. It contains incredible nuggets of wisdom, because the best advice you can ever receive comes from an All-Knowing, All -Loving God.

ACTIONS SPEAK

One of my all time favorite sayings is: "Your actions are so loud, I can't hear what you are saying!"

About 20 years ago, Dina, one of my dear friends today taught me a life-changing lesson. It is one that I have been conscious of ever since.

Dina is a very busy doctor; one of the hardest working people I know. At the time of this lesson she had three young children. She worked Monday through Friday way over eight hours a day and came home to be a wife and mother. I would tell her, "I'm going to call and we'll get together"—but I rarely did.

With three kids of my own, life was busy for me too.

Regardless of my distractions, my words were "empty" to her. Why? Because my actions did not live up to my words. I saw her at church and the conversation we exchanged went something like this. "Let's get together. I miss seeing you!" I said.

Dina, smiled and replied, "Okay!" Later that afternoon she called and said she needed to talk with me.

"No problem," I responded, wondering what was up.

Thus began a hard, candid conversation. Her next comment hit me like a ton of bricks.

Dina hesitated, then continued, "Your words are meaningless to me at this point, because you seldom call and we rarely get together!"

Since words of encouragement are my number one love language, you have to understand how painful this was to hear from someone whom I considered to be a close friend. Her blunt statement was like a knock-out punch that rocked me for about two weeks.

I cried. I prayed. And after several days of staying to myself, thinking about what she said and reflecting on our friendship, I realized her words were absolutely correct.

There is a saying that I have found to be true: "Truth may hurt, but it never harms." Well, this time it really did hurt. Through prayer, God began to heal my heart and show me His grace–and also what I needed to do. The Bible is the best way the Lord speaks to me and I searched Scripture for comfort and answers.

Two verses in particular seemed to jump right off the pages. Proverbs 27:6 says, *"Faithful are the wounds of a friend, but the kisses of an enemy are deceitful."* And in 1 John 3:18 I read, *"My little children, let us not love in word or in tongue, but in deed and in truth."*

BOOM! That hit me right between the eyes!

There were several other passages that applied to this particular situation, but these short verses were all it took for me to go and visit my friend. I needed to ask for her forgiveness, which she immediately gave, but I realized it didn't stop there!

I began to take a long, introspective look at my relationships to see if this applied to other friendships in my life—and it did! As hard as I try, I still sometimes fail at always having my words and actions line up, and it is a matter I am constantly examining. Unplanned circumstances of daily living often invade our well-intended plans, but I want to remind anyone reading this that *actions are who we are!*

Talk is cheap, and words roll easily off our tongues. However, if there is no follow-through, what we say becomes hollow and meaningless.

To this very day, the honesty of my friend, God's Word, and self-reflection are things for which I am forever grateful.

AN OUTPOURING OF COMPASSION

"You can never plan your schedule around when a person is going to die."

These are the exact words I told many of my friends when my mother passed away. I wanted them to know I understood that they couldn't be there, but I knew they loved me.

My mother went to be with the Lord on April 16, 2014, just before Easter. It was the week when many of my friends who had kids were on spring break and enjoying family trips. It was so sweet of the people who called to tell me they regretted not being able to attend my mom's funeral. I certainly understood. That week was NOT the time that I would have been able to identify who really loved me and cared. Certainly, those were devastating days filled with sadness—and now, looking back, it seems all a blur.

Burying my mom has continued to validate and teach me that "Nothing can happen through you until it happens to you."

First hand experience is key. Actually, it is the personal action of lacing your shoes and traveling down a road you have never walked before that teaches you…"Wow! So that is what this is like!"

I can remember when Thomas was five and diagnosed with Type 1 diabetes, a disease for which there is no cure. I learned an invaluable lesson about compassion and encouragement. There were people who rushed to our side and extended heart-felt empathy I had *never* before experienced. Individuals I never thought would do so responded to the pain of our devastation.

Thomas was so young and so sick. He doesn't remember the *"outpouring!"* (I wish he could.) It makes me think of the book of Acts and the description of the early church. In chapter 4, it details how the believers took care of each other. Verses 32-37 describe how they did what was required so "that there were no needy persons among them."

With Thomas, the care and concern we felt continued for months and years. Shortly after his diagnosis, when the shock had diminished and I could get my "legs" back, I sat up, literally all night, thanking God for the "flood of love and compassion." At the same time, I also felt "terrible regret" over my lack of sensitivity in the past for others in their hour of pain! But I have learned to thank God for our storm. Because it happened in our home, far better love and encouragement can now happen through me. The same holds true in the days and years that are ahead, as I have now lived through the loss of my dear mom.

My point is simple: Pain is something that happens to everyone on the planet!

Many times we can't predict when it will strike or in what form it will be, but it is 100% certain that if you live you will experience pain.

Unfortunately, we can become stuck in the anguish. Trust me, I am not referring to grief here. Grief is a natural process we all encounter and must allow God to "carry us through." But He also wants to weave love into our hearts, which should lead us to acts of compassion for others who are hurting. His plan is that we help someone else who is walking in grief and heartache and help "carry the load" and shoulder their burden.

Let me give you just one example of an "outpouring" of encouragement that I have been a recipient of. Several months after my mother passed, I had a dear friend call. She expressed that she and others wanted to have a dinner at her house. They wanted to invite guests over for a "love dinner"—to love on me after my mom's death.

Many who came to the dinner were not able to attend the funeral. This gesture did a beautiful thing to my heart and spirit! They lived out loud Romans 12:15: *"Rejoice with those who rejoice, weep with those who weep."*

I encourage you, if you have not walked some of life's paths of pain and would like to be a more uplifting and compassionate person, look to those around you. Learn from them and even ask them questions. We can all gain so much insight from others, especially the individuals of whom we can truly say, "Your actions are so loud that I can't hear what you are saying!"

When you experience a strong dose of love during a time

of sadness and suffering, it is something you never forget. The messages I have received from others through their actions contained "a piece of them." Because they, too, have traveled a similar path and know how to minister to the hurting.

When you walk through pain, make note of how others minister to you. God wastes nothing. You never know when He may give you the opportunity to show compassion to another who is on the road behind you.

TELLING IT LIKE IT IS

While it is often difficult for adults to speak the truth, it's certainly no problem for children. I'm sure you can give me an example or two.

It you're looking for blunt honesty, just ask a five-year-old.

Tucker is my oldest and only nephew and Brewer is our oldest son. I think they deserve a lot of grace in their lives because they were the first born. If you have more than one child, I'm sure you'll agree that as parents we learn a library of knowledge with our first.

Both of these fellows have given us a lot to laugh about, especially when they were young. I remember when Tucker was five and was watching his babysitter, Joanne, change my niece's diaper. As he stared intently, he looked up at Joanne and innocently, but seriously asked, "Joanne, why is Lauren's butt in the front?"

I'm sure you can smile at this observation.

Not long after that I remember Brewer being in a stifling hot elevator with Bill's mom when he suddenly blurted out,

"Gramma, why is your face melting?"

Don't you just love how children have no inhibitions and say exactly what they are thinking? I have known for a very long time, if you ever want a reality check, all you have to do is ask a child. They will unapologetically tell you the *truth.*

Speaking the truth in love is something we all need in our lives. I am so appreciative of the moments when I am disheveled and someone reaches out to fix my hair, or discreetly tells me I have pepper stuck in my teeth (I think that comes with age).

These are appearance flaws, and most friends are willing to help you in those areas. But what about our heart flaws? Do you have loved ones who will step up to the plate?

Honesty and accountability are things we should all seek—it's how we grow and become stronger.

A we mature in our Christian walk, the Bible tells us, *"We should no longer be children, tossed to and fro and carried about with every wind of doctrine, by the trickery of men, in the cunning craftiness of deceitful plotting, but, speaking the truth in love, may grow up in all things into Him who is the head—Christ"* (Ephesians 4:14-15).

WISE COUNSEL

Several years ago, I took a step of faith. As I studied Scripture I knew I still needed to improve, and change needed to occur. I had blind spots, as we all do. God led me to seek the advice of a dear and wise woman named Bebe. We spent many hours sharing and praying together. She was a true confidant who gently and kindly pointed out some areas I needed to address and open myself up to examination and change. This was the beginning of an exciting new "growth period" for me!

During this time, I sought the advice and wisdom of several other friends. Thankfully, all of these individuals were gentle and shared their weaknesses and struggles with me. Not only was this a great source of encouragement, but it let me know that I wasn't stranded alone on an island, nor was I the only one who had ever gone through something like this.

I then took it a step further to seek advice from a recommended, qualified Christian counselor.

I cannot begin to express to you how opening the windows of my life to trusted Christian friends and wise counsel has taken me on a path of extreme spiritual growth.

Never before had I realized how beneficial it would be to ask a person to take a close look and point out the weak areas they saw—and then love me as I changed them. The process is ongoing, but oh, how far I have journeyed.

If you feel stagnant, as if your feet are stuck in mud, let me motivate you to take a leap of faith. Pray and allow God to guide you to wise counsel. Learn to be uncomfortable, because that is where growth occurs.

I have never bought into the saying, "Too old to change." To me, this is a cop-out and a pride issue. True transformation requires God, honesty, desire, courage, accountability, encouragement, and being uncomfortable. As you seek new growth, remember, "If you do what you have always done, you will get what you've always gotten." Today, try something different!

MIMIC ME

Now that we have an empty nest, I am blessed to interact with "adopted babies" as practice for my own grandchildren someday. I am amazed as I watch these precious "little things!"

A one-year-old I have "adopted" mimics everything I do. The other night at dinner he was being held by his own dad, but directly looking at Bill and crossing his arms just like my husband. We all saw it and began to laugh. It was cute to see a baby mimic an adult. Earlier in the day when I was caring for him, I would stick out my tongue and make funny faces. Instantly, he shadowed everything I did. I loved every minute of having his full attention and watching him squint his face to work hard at duplicating my actions. I think when my kids were young, I was so green at the parenting thing, and tired at times, I didn't see all the mimicking or enjoy it as much as I do now! Perhaps the reason is, I am much more rested!

Here's the point. If you are young parents, growing your family, never overlook the fact that kids want to be a mirror image of you.

They are little "sponges" with acute "radars" picking up signals, body language, and all of our actions.

They are watching, learning, and *duplicating* our every

move. Remember, we have much to do with shaping who they are and what they become!

With this being said, I daily thank God for His grace! I certainly know that I haven't been the perfect role model, but thank goodness we have a heavenly Father who covers our mistakes! The one thing we did right was to give our children daily encouragement, and I am thrilled to see them mimicking that to others.

TOUCHY SUBJECTS

"Be sensitive please!" That's what I feel like screaming at some people—and I have to ask the Lord to bridle my tongue. Nothing can get a rise out of me faster than when an individual is not keenly aware and understanding of someone else's feelings.

In such times, when I could melt steel, it is a true test for me to obey the advice to *"be angry and sin not"* (Ephesians 4:26).

I constantly strive to be considerate of those around me and continually ask the Lord to help me *do unto others as I would have them do unto me* (see Matthew 7:12).

The Bible offers this counsel: *"Like one who takes away a garment on a cold day, or like vinegar poured on a wound, is one who sings songs to a heavy heart"* (Proverbs 25:20 NIV).

You might stop and ask, "Who on earth would intentionally sing a song to a heavy heart in order to hurt them?"

Sadly, it happens all the time and people just don't realize the damage they are inflicting. There are individuals who are deeply wounded and hurting, and out of not knowing what to say, or being nervous, "make light" of the situation. We should avoid this at all cost, no matter how trivial it might seem.

I learned the "insensitivity" lesson many years ago, first-hand, from my own pain. The one thing I can tell you is that I, too, was not mindful of my comments to someone else's anguish until, "I wore the shoes!"

Comments individuals made during the first few months after Thomas was diagnosed with Type 1 diabetes were unintentionally painful. I now see they were well-meaning but, at the time, it was like they were "stabbing my heart" with a butcher knife, one forged with jagged edges. I know that is a graphic description of the pain, but bear with me. There is a lesson to be learned.

For the first several months after Thomas was diagnosed, I was devastated in so many ways. Type 1 is not a death sentence, but it is a "chronic disease" that is life-altering.

For weeks I was racked with emotional pain and fatigue. I cannot tell you how many times I heard: "Be thankful!" "Be thankful it is not cancer!" "Be thankful he is alive!" "Be thankful..."

If I heard it once, I heard it a hundred times in some form or another. Each time it felt like another stab wound. I spent my days trying to stay strong and not constantly cry. I was scared, hurt, sad, and in shock, wanting the best possible outcome for our son. I had to get past the initial emotion before getting to the "be thankful" stage.

Today, if you are seeking to offer words of encouragement to a wounded person, acknowledge their pain and let them know that your heart hurts for them.

HELPING, OR HURTING?

Recently, I was with a mom and her teenage daughter. The young woman was dealing with a broken heart (rejection) and was devastated. If you are an adult, you know what that can be like, especially if you are female—and even more so if you have a daughter. As adults, we often have a "helicopter view," seeing from above, based on experience, knowing things get better in time, and sometimes that causes us to be insensitive to the here-and-now pain. Heartbreak at any age can be "earth shattering."

It only took a matter of minutes before this sweet, broken-hearted teen was "taken out at the knees" with comments from well-intentioned adults. Words such as, "Oh, you'll be fine! Just give it time!" Or, "You're still young!"

Then these outsiders followed up with stories of their own daughter's broken heart, going into way too many details about how she now has a wonderful boyfriend. While all this may have been true, they were just "trying to put a band-aid on a fresh, gushing wound."

Watching from the sidelines, it almost seemed they were making "light" of the young girl's misery.

As soon as the women walked away, the girl burst into tears. Wow! You could see it coming. The adults left the room thinking they had actually helped!

TRUE COMPASSION

I believe that some individuals, because they are older and have the mindset of "been there, done that," can be almost prideful and show little compassion in dealing with the "here and now."

When people are hurting, especially if it is a recent emotional wound, be very careful not to bring a "quick, silver-lining statement!" Or, if you have never truly experienced what they are going through, please don't glibly say, "I know how you feel."

If you have not walked down their exact path, you really do not know! Even if you have traveled a harder road, this is not the time to elaborate on your story and how you made it through. Seriously, people who are in the throes of deep pain (doesn't matter if you feel what they are feeling or not), are not so much looking for illustrations, they are needing compassion. They are waiting to hear, "I am so sorry. I know you are hurting!"

Acknowledge their pain. You might say, "I love you and I will just sit here with you!" A hug, a touch, even a tear, is better than a gusher of words when you have no idea if they can even comprehend the situation of the moment. Again, you do not have to have experienced their pain to be caring and sensitive.

Even if the trouble seems trivial, don't discount someone's deep-felt feelings. If it is a young person, remember it is a part of growing up.

Kids, no matter the age or source of their anguish, need to

have their feelings validated and not swept under the rug or discounted because of their youth. They are watching our every move, listening to our every word, and learning from us how to treat others who are wounded. Even if we haven't been treated fairly in our own time of despair, learn from it and be a better example.

There is so much suffering in our world, both physical and emotional. It is a part of life that needs more attention. When it is our turn to face a trial, how wonderful it is to find a friend who will just listen—and only speak what the Lord leads them to share.

I pray you will pay attention to your words and actions! As an adult, it is extremely important for you to model and show your heart of compassion. Remember, when a soul is hurting, it's not about you! It is all about them!

The best encouragement is to show how much you care.

NOTES FOR YOUR SCORECARD

- Opinions are just that—opinions.
- Make sure your words are accompanied by actions.
- Speak truth in love by helping, not hurting.
- Since children mimic you, be careful what you say and do.
- Encouragement includes being sensitive to the feelings of others.
- We grow by being honest and accountable.
- Empathize with the current situation of a friend, without talking about your own past struggles.

Tee #15
Determination

Certain outcomes happen in golf one hundred percent of the time. If a golfer fails to get the ball to the hole when he putts, it doesn't have a chance of going in. Even if it is only a centimeter too short; it's not going in.

When our kids play golf, I have to bite my lip when their putting consistently leaves the ball short of the hole, especially if they are putting for a birdie.

After watching hundreds of rounds of golf, I can honestly say our children shoot their best scores when they are at least getting their putts to the hole consistently. I have found if the first putt goes past the hole, they usually make it coming back.

For whatever reason, sometimes a golfer is so caught up in other distractions on the greens that they don't recognize they are leaving their putts short. Often, they are "fearful" of running the ball too far past the hole. Or maybe they think that if they run it by too much, they may have a very difficult putt coming back.

While I don't claim to be a great authority on golf, I see the parallels of life to the sport.

On the "green" of life, I often ask myself a series of questions:

- Am I coming up short?
- Am I getting things to the "hole" and giving myself the best chance for a good score in the "game of life"?
- Do I even recognize when I am coming up "short" and not being consistent in delivering the ball where it needs to be to have a chance at success?

Maybe I/we/you need to examine factors that we can control—and not only recognize where we may be leaving things short, but have a determination to do something about it—resulting in a better score in life!

Let me ask some specific questions to help make the point. I use the word "we," to include myself:

- Are we faithful to keep our word?
- Can we be counted on?
- Do we return calls and, not only return them, but do so in a timely manner?
- Do we spend our time on matters that will bring improvement?
- Do we stop to say thank you?
- Are we willing to go the extra mile for someone who can never repay us?
- Are we generous only to people who are in our "inner circle?"
- Do we get enough sleep?
- What do we allow our eyes to see?
- Do we surround ourselves with people who sharpen us?
- Are we achieving only halfway? Half-heartedly? Have we set the bar too low?

- Do we get up with a purpose or are we plodding along through the motions with no plan?
- What are we feeding ourselves physically? Mentally? Spiritually?

  – The list could go on and on.

Make sure today you take time to step off the "course" and examine your actions. Take ruthlessly honest notes. Is there a place I/you/we are coming up short?

The degree to which you are honest with yourself is the degree that you can exert change.

For me, it has been shoring up the little things that has made a huge difference—taking the time out of my "to do" list to assist someone else or stop and express my gratitude. To show genuine appreciation, not with just a verbal thank you, but with a lunch date or "hand-written note."

One of the biggest changes for me personally has been following through on my determination to get up earlier and read more, understanding that I have to seek knowledge! I've become a life-long learner and am eager to become more teachable. Laying down my pride and realizing I don't have all the answers, I spend my time learning and knowing more! I have found on the Back 9 it's the most unhappy people who dread change. If everything remained the status quo, we would only see moths, and no beautiful butterflies! Change is the evidence of growth.

As the British theologian, John Henry Newman, wrote, "Growth is the only evidence of life."

GOD STORIES

I love to hear people tell their "God stories"—especially those that involve their strong determination and require giant leaps of faith. They encourage and inspire me to "go and do likewise" by taking steps in a direction without knowing the outcome. This means trusting God and knowing He "has you."

In the Bible there are countless such stories. For example, Noah obeying God and building the ark (which took many years before the great flood). It was his unwavering faith and trust that saved his entire family. The same factors were at work when Moses led the children of Israel out of slavery and toward the Promised Land.

Such stories exist today.

I have watched many friends take bold, determined steps of faith in their lives, such as Henry and Celia Deneen.

Henry was a successful attorney and judge in Columbia, South Carolina, with four young children when he trusted and honored the call of God to pick up and leave Columbia and a very successful career. He and his family moved to the west coast where he attended Golden Gate Seminary, saying goodby to their creature comforts—nice house, family, friends, careers, and incomes.

This call of God didn't stop in California; it continued after seminary to missions in France, then back to Columbia, and on to Colorado where he became the CEO of Greater European Mission (GEM). All the while, his wife, Celia, and their children, Lee, Laura, Leslie, and Layna, cheerfully followed him and the Lord's leading in his life.

It has been so encouraging and inspiring to watch the obedience and fruit that has resulted from such a walk of faith. Their children have pursued their own paths in law, music, sports, and education. Celia is still impacting kids as she has always done by being a guidance counselor in a public school.

It is marvelous to see how God has blessed this family, providing for them as their lives have zigzagged all over the map while trusting the Lord to guide them. The cool thing is the countless lives that God is touching through all six of them.

Bill and I had been married just a year when we moved to Columbia. It was Henry and Celia who reached out to us and became our friends. Their influence and encouragement prompted us to not just occupy a pew in church each Sunday, but to become involved in the work of the Lord.

The point I am making is that deciding to trust God and follow His leading may not always make sense to you or to those around you. Acting in faith is all that matters.

Without trust in God as our provider, we are limited to our own resources. But when we launch out in faith, the sky's the limit!

It is never too late to place your complete confidence in your heavenly Father. Determine to:

- Trust God by daring to be vulnerable.
- Trust God by asking yourself, "What do I need to trust Him for?"

- Trust God's character—and not any particular outcome.
- Trust God even when you don't understand.
- Trust God by being obedient even when it doesn't make sense.
- Trust God as you define the steps you need to take to make changes.
- Trust God, even if it means rewriting your "map"—and the Lord adds a zigzag or two.
- Trust God as you take action and "pull the trigger!"

By your commitment to do these things, your life will become richer and it will allow you to be used by God more significantly. There is amazing, wonder-working power in earnestly seeking the Lord.

Remember, *"But without faith it is impossible to please Him, for he who comes to God must believe that He is, and that He is a rewarder of those who diligently seek Him"* (Hebrews 11:6).

THIS IS HOW I ROLL

I was more than shocked when a former U.S. congressman, who had been involved in a "sexting" scandal, thought it was perfectly acceptable to run for another high office. He defended his actions of the past and present by glibly stating, "This is how I roll."

Thankfully, the public didn't see it his way and the politician was forced to drop out of the race.

In light of how sickening his view on repeating his

indiscretions was to me, I turned to the pages of Scripture to see how Jesus intended for believers "to roll."

The Son of God said, *"I am the vine, you are the branches. He who abides in Me, and I in him, bears much fruit; for without Me you can do nothing"* (John 15:5-6).

The last part of the passage grabs my attention—and *keeps* it. The way God desires for us to "roll" is with *Him.* He doesn't say we can do some things without Him; it is much more direct than that. Unless the Lord is with us, we can *"do nothing."*

Now is the time to pause and think about these words. It's easy to become so preoccupied with our busy schedules that we put Jesus on the back burner, perhaps giving Him a "head fake" here and there with our attention and time. We read our Bible occasionally, or grab it at night just before we wind down and go to sleep when everything else in our day has taken priority. We do it so we can check it off our list. We attend church on Sunday out of routine, because that's what all "Christians" do—the Sunday thing. As a result we are going through meaningless motion. Nothing we do really counts because it was done in our own strength.

I believe that when the Lord speaks of bearing fruit, it means the significance and impact we can have on others for Him. This can include uplifting a hurting soul, offering a helping hand, or countless other meaningful expressions of love.

If we have been in the Word (the Bible) and spent time with Jesus, especially in the first part of our day, it allows us to have our "focus" on the Lord and His plan for us.

My mom always said, "You cannot give what you don't possess!"—and if you met with the King of the Universe in the first part of your morning, then you are capable of talking to anybody throughout your day.

As His branches, we are attached to the "vine." The communication is there and, as a result, we can be "aware and alert" of the doors *He* opens for us every day—and hopefully there will be no missed opportunities. When this happens, the result will be one of abundance—"bearing much FRUIT!"

I must be honest and admit, I have been good about this at times and very bad at others. Whether we like it or not, if we are not disciplined, diligent, and determined in our walk with Christ, the fast "roll" can become slow and off course—and suddenly you are "rolling" in a completely wrong direction; in a totally different fairway!

If you have read my blogs and earlier book, you know that there were years when my fruit bearing was rather sparse because of "people pleasing" instead of God pleasing. But once I made a determination to spend more time making certain the Lord was my number one priority, I could physically see the "fruit" become evident.

It is so easy to let outside factors stand in the way of our relationship with God. It took some convincing and true self-examination to really realize my "totem pole" had the wrong "stack." God was second. And if He is second, He might as well be *last!*

Fruit on the Vine

Allow me to give you a meaningful, example of bearing fruit.

As a result of a commitment and determination, I spend time with God each morning. This takes place very early and sometimes lasts longer than expected. I have to wake up before daylight so I can still accomplish all I need to do, thus a major sacrifice on my part is sleep. The benefits, however, far outweigh the sacrifice!

In these early hours I have been able to more clearly hear God speak to my spirit. I have become attuned to recognize this feeling; which I can only describe as one of thirst or hunger (not a voice). Some person's name will pop into my mind. Over time, I have come to realize that the name, along with the feeling, go together. I pray for that individual and follow it up with a card, text, or phone call.

Last year, while I was traveling, the name of my friend, Terri, rested heavily on my heart. I prayed for her and then texted her! It was just minutes before I received a response. Her text went something like this, "Wow! You really have no idea how hearing from you came at just the right time. It has encouraged me far more than you know. Thank you!"

Then a few minutes later, she texted again and said, "I want to make sure you know how much this helped me and the timing was perfect!"

I was not looking for any response. But God in His faithfulness reassured me through her, "You are hearing Me correctly, so keep on rolling!"

This is how the Lord intends for us to roll as His children.

If we are sensitive and connected to His will, His timing is perfect in our lives (and others) and we can be used by Him to help people—even through a simple, quick text.

I encourage you to make sure that God is number one in all you do! Remain in Him and you will readily see opportunities to reach out to others, thus bearing fruit!

GOD'S WAY OF PARENTING

Determination is the driving force that cements marriages and families together. And it is a necessary parenting tool.

I loved reading the life story of the iconic evangelist Billy Graham's wife, Ruth. She was an absolutely amazing woman and a true role model. She was born in China to missionary parents and met Billy at Wheaton College at the age of 20.

Ruth was strong, loving, humorous, independent, prayerful, strict, resolute and unwavering in her beliefs. What attracted Billy to her? He commented, "It was not what she said, but what she was."

She shared an incident involving their son Franklin when he was a child (one of their five). He was known for being very rebellious and once got into a rather boisterous fight with his sister in the car. Ruth promptly pulled off the North Carolina highway, put him in the trunk and drove him home!

Reading that made me laugh, but today she probably would have been put in jail for child abuse! How times have changed in parenting. Of course, I am totally against any form of cruelty to children, and so was Ruth. I realize that the "bad, abusive parents" have made our culture gravitate to the extreme in protecting our kids, sometimes to their detriment.

In the words of an old saying, "One bad apple can spoil the whole bunch!"

Our nation's pendulum has swung so far in sheltering kids (who are *all* immature and lack experience) that it has lumped the good parents with the bad.

I grieve over the extremes that have gone so far to safeguard our children that caring, concerned parents have to walk on "egg shells" and can't be mothers and fathers as the Bible teaches.

You don't have to tell a child/toddler to be selfish and self-centered. It comes naturally. As Proverbs 22:15 states, *"Foolishness is bound up in the heart of a child; the rod of discipline will drive it far from him."*

This "foolishness" is common in all of us. On the other hand, discipline is something that has to be trained and taught. It amazes me that the expectation of our culture has moved more and more toward society, schools/teachers, and government to discipline our offspring. Is it any wonder we are in such trouble as a nation?

Training, discipline, and nurturing of our children were intended by God to begin and be practiced in the home.

People scratch their heads and complain about the growing violence and disrespect that exists in younger generations. It's time we become determined to get back to basics.

The Bible is a storehouse of guidance when it comes to parenting. Proverbs 19:18 tells us, *"Chasten your son while there is hope, and do not set your heart on his destruction."* While Colossians 3:21 counsels, *"Fathers do not provoke your children, lest they become discouraged."*

When you study the *whole* Bible you begin to see how God intends for parents to raise children. It first starts with mothers and fathers seeking a heart for God and having the "fruit of the Spirit" themselves—*"love, joy, peace, longsuffering, kindness, goodness, faithfulness, gentleness, self-control"* (Galatians 5:22-23).

It is intended for parents to raise their sons and daughters out of a desire and heart to please God. When this happens, there will be a healthy view on how we should evoke and administer discipline to the young people we are responsible for. All the while, when we make mistakes, we must acknowledge them to God and our kids.

Looking at Franklin Graham's life today and his worldwide impact with *Samaritan's Purse*, tells me his mother and dad did a whole lot of things RIGHT, with God at the helm of their home.

DETERMINED TO WALK

One of the favorite experiences God brought into my life on the Back 9 was the time of helping a young couple with their baby! I am not yet a grandparent but have found this to be a rewarding ministry and mostly a whole lot of fun. Needless to say, the Lord has carved a special place in my heart for Frank, Ericka and little I.V., and Hank.

Ericka is an ER nurse and I was able to keep I.V. and Hank for several hours at a time while she and Frank were working.

It was a ball!

When I.V. celebrated his first birthday, I enjoyed being included in the party plans. It was a blast seeing him take those faltering, first "baby steps," maneuvering around our coffee table and crawling to the fireplace.

You don't remember it, but as a baby, you learned to walk by pulling yourself up and falling down—not just once, but hundreds of times. Determined, you tried again, and again, and again. Eventually you walked; then you ran and even jumped!

I closely observed little I.V.'s never-ending attempts to walk. He didn't cry, or even get mad. Plain and simply, he was fueled with a tankfull of determination—and attempted walking in a variety of ways.

Wouldn't it be wonderful if we treated all of our efforts in life the same way?

The major difference between people who succeed and those who don't is found in how they handle their failure. Both groups fail. However, it's what you do next after you fail that matters most. The ones who take responsibility for themselves, learn from their mistakes and determine not to repeat them. Maintaining a positive, determined attitude while learning, is a key to success.

God created us to walk; He also created us to achieve —but not without failure. It's how we respond to those missteps and errors that ultimately defines our success.

Along with determination, we simply must take *responsibility* for our failures. Sure there can be outside circumstances and people who may contribute to our problems, but we must realize life doesn't always work out the way we'd like it to. Things aren't always fair; those around us don't always have the best motives (selfish motives affect others–usually adversely). No one is going to live your life for you.

It is up to your determination and relying on the ultimate help and direction available from your heavenly Father.

If you are caught in a discouraging situation, ask yourself, "Will I be responsible?" and "Will I look to my Maker—the One who created me to walk—the One who has a plan and purpose for me to fulfill?"

Please don't make it your habit to live with a "blame-storming" mentality. And be determined not to point an accusing finger at the unfairness of life. The Bible clearly states that God causes the sun to rise on both the evil and the good, and He sends rain to the just and unjust. We can't allow ourselves to get bogged down in failures and what life throws our way. Instead, we need to understand, as Benjamin Franklin wisely said, "Those things that hurt, instruct."

Perhaps we all need to take the time to once again watch a baby trying to walk. See their tenacity, optimism, and pure grit. Then realize that God didn't create us merely to *learn* to walk, but to take confident, bold steps and achieve great things on our journey—to run our race in order to obtain the prize.

As it is written, *"And now, Israel* [insert your name], *what does the Lord your God require of you, but to fear the Lord your God, to walk in all His ways and to love Him, to serve the Lord your God with all your heart and with all your soul, and to keep the commands of the Lord and His statutes which I command you today for your good?"* (Deuteronomy 10:12-13).

Is that your determination?

NOTES FOR YOUR SCORECARD

- Determine to avoid "coming up short."
- Look for the "God stories" all around you.
- The Lord intends for you to "roll" by bearing fruit for Him.
- Determine to follow God's guidance for parenting.
- Learning to walk requires hundreds of attempts and failures.
- Take responsibility for your mistakes, and try again.
- Success requires determination, optimism, and tenacity.
- It is what we do next after failure that matters most.

Tee #16
Gratitude

I am a firm believer that every person who steps into our lives is placed there by God's design.

Many know Sterling Sharpe as a five-time Pro Bowl wide receiver during his six years with the Green Bay Packers. To our family, however, he is a valued friend.

We've had the blessing of knowing Sterling for more than 30 years. Our relationship with him came from my husband, Bill, who played football with Sterling at the University of South Carolina. The friendship has grown deep through the bond our children have built with him around golf, especially our daughter, Collins.

As our children were growing up, all three would go to the golf course for long days of practice and play. Our boys had many friends who played the sport, so a foursome was always readily available even at the age of 9 and 10, especially with their closest buddies, Will and JB. Not so for Collins. In fact, there were no girls even close to her age at our club who played the game or stayed for the long hours that Collins would put in. Until our daughter developed her game (learned how to keep up and play fast), she was never included in the boys' foursomes.

Sterling became Collins playing partner. I will never forget Collins being around the age of 9 and calling me from the

Spring Valley Country Club to tell me that she played 18 holes with Sterling. He had seen Collins on the course by herself many times while the boys played a foursome in front of her. One hot, muggy day he picked her up to play 18. Not only did she have a blast and feel extremely fortunate, but she got to ride in his cart while the boys walked. It was 100 degrees outside, so that was a welcome bonus.

That day, a friendship/mentoring relationship was born. Most people know Sterling for his record-breaking years at Green Bay or as a television commentator, but I have gained a special fondness for this huge, smart, kind, successful African-American man—not to mention that he earned not one, but two degrees from the University of South Carolina.

Sterling not only took my daughter under his wing, but developed a strong relationship of caring, offering advice, listening, and keeping up with Collins for the years that followed.

She truly considers him a best friend and he has proven to be just that!

A True Samaritan

Several years ago Sterling was in charge of introducing his brother, Shannon (former tight end for the Baltimore Ravens and the Denver Broncos), when Shannon was inducted into the NFL Hall of Fame.

I can remember being in Hilton Head, South Carolina, at the State Amateur golf tournament, planning our evening around watching this event on television. The speech that

Sterling presented was everything we expected, and more. I've watched the YouTube playback several times to glean and appreciate where the Sharpe brothers came from and how their lives were shaped—so much different than how Bill and I or our kids grew up.

This former Pro-Bowl player has a beautiful wife and daughter of his own, and his work requires him to travel constantly. But somehow he has always made time to mentor, listen, and give strong, sound advice to Collins.

To my husband and me, Sterling Sharpe is a modern day Good Samaritan.

He is a prime example of the principles I want to share with you in this chapter. They include spreading love through unexpected acts of kindness, giving without any expectation of return, thanking God when He turns your attention to the needs of others, and being grateful for the priceless gift of love.

Allow me to tell the story of the Bible's version of another person like Sterling.

Once, when Jesus was confronted by the experts concerning Hebrew law, He was asked what we should do to inherit eternal life. The Lord replied, *"'You shall love the Lord your God with all your heart, with all your soul, with all your strength, and with all your mind,' and 'your neighbor as yourself'"* (Luke 10:27).

Jesus goes on to relate the story of a wounded man left to die on the side of the road after being attacked and beaten by robbers. A priest, and then a Levite, both traveling from Jerusalem to Jericho, passed by, ignored the wounded man and crossed over to the other side of the road. Next came a

Samaritan who saw the victim lying there helpless. He took "pity" on him and bandaged his wounds. Then he lifted the stranger onto his donkey, took him to an inn, paid for his care, and went on his way, only to say he would return to check on him and pay any other expenses.

In biblical times the Samaritans were despised by the Jews and would not have been seen as heroes in any story. This was not the ending they expected to hear from Jesus.

Unfortunately, today is not much different. In the South it seems there are still traces of stigma regarding blacks and whites associating in certain settings. To others it may seem odd that this big guy would befriend our daughter. I can almost see the raised eyebrows—a black man mentoring a young white girl!

In my opinion, Sterling Sharpe is a present day Samaritan who deserves our gratitude. He took pity on Collins when she was nine, even letting her ride in his golf cart. He championed her cause, bolstered her confidence, checking on her progress many times. Recently, when Collins suffered some setbacks and felt emotionally dead, he picked her up, bandaged her wounds, and carried her forward. He has literally cared for her to the extent of using his experience in broadcast journalism, which was Collins' major in college, and taken her to "new heights." Sterling has treated her like his own child and demonstrated what it means to "love your neighbor as yourself."

SPREADING THE SUGAR

I love to watch young kids doing great things in athletics,

especially if it involves sportsmanship, random acts of kindness, and friendship. Where is ESPN when you need them? I would broadcast these scenarios to the masses! I like to call it, "Spreading the sugar!"

The reason I talk so much about golf is because it has been such a huge part of our lives, and the Lord has used it to teach me so much.

A continual lesson has been that of giving, receiving, and why we need to be thankful. It has come in the form of gifts of encouragement, acts of service, and friendship. Our kids have been the recipients countless times.

Let me share these three examples.

In 2006, we were in Hilton Head, South Carolina, at the state's Junior Golf Championship. It was over 95 degrees and Thomas, (14 at that time) our middle son and diabetic, had an afternoon tee time. I cannot begin to describe how miserable the conditions were—hot, humid, and very sticky with no breeze. It was the second day of the tournament and I walked ahead to hole number 2 which was a par 5. I looked back at the tee, to see someone standing next to Thomas and holding his bag. I walked over, straining to see who it was. I discovered it was his friend and fellow competitor, McQuen, who had played in the morning round. Then, after lunch, McQuen came out to "loop" for Thomas." This a golf term that means someone else is carrying your bag.

This act of kindness was true sportsmanship.

Another memorable sugar-spreading memory took place when our daughter, Collins, was 16 and in the Carolina's

Match Play in Camden. Her friend, Stephen, volunteered to caddy multiple rounds and days, giving up his time to practice and compete, just to help her. These acts of kindness made wonderful memories.

By the way, Collins ended up winning the tournament and Thomas made a "Double Eagle" on #2, the hole McQuen joined him on to loop.

THE "THREE AMIGOS"

The third example happened when we were at "The Porter Cup Amateur Championship" in Buffalo, New York. It is an event that has been staged since 1959 and has a rich heritage. To say the least, we were thrilled that Thomas was invited to play. Phil Mickelson won the event in 1990 and some of the tournament's other past participants include Tiger Woods, Davis Love II, and David Duval.

Thomas actually got to stay in the host home of the tournament director, Steve Denn and his wife, Susan. They were awesome and treated him like a king. Every day Susan would pack extra Gatorade and Thomas' favorite, vanilla wafers and peanut butter, and bring them to him. The tournament is a 4-day event and every moment was special.

On the final day, Thomas played with two really great guys, Patrick and Nick. They were outstanding young golfers, but neither had played their "A" game, so they were not in the final group.

As I walked up to the first tee to observe, there was a rather large crowd gathered, but what stood out to me were three young guys (in their twenties) with matching green shirts. On the front of the shirt was a picture of their friend, Pat, who was in Thomas' threesome. When the announcers called Pat's name, they broke out into chants, cheers and applause which, for me, was quite refreshing. No one ever really cheers a whole lot in golf. People say "Shot," "Good shot," or "Putt" under their breath and clap very softly most of the time.

Being a former cheerleader, I would love to shout on the golf course when something good happens or maybe even jump, but I refrain, mostly to keep from embarrassing our kids!

The young men in green shirts, I now fondly call "The Three Amigos." Their enthusiasm was contagious and before long I started to cheer for Thomas and Nick as well. By the third hole I was joining in, to the point that I told them, "I didn't get the memo about the matching green shirts!"

Guess what? They offered me one! I replied, "Seriously?"

They said, "Yes! We are Pat's Fan Club and we have shirts in the car and will get you one."

By the fifth hole we were cheering for Pat, Thomas, and Nick for any good shot they hit. At the turn, I got my green shirt, which I proudly wore!

Of course, I had to ask questions about the "Three Amigos," Ryan, Nick, and Matt, and their friendship with Pat. They told me they had been buddies since the fifth grade and, as much as they could, they came out to support their friend. I saw this as a true example of living out Romans 15:2: *"Each of us should please our neighbors for their good, to build them up"* (NIV).

I was so amazed by the out-of-the-ordinary bond these young men had! It spoke volumes to me as to how all of us could better support our friends. They even rooted for Thomas and owned him for the day as well as Nick—demonstrating Leviticus 19:34: *"The stranger who dwells among you shall be to you as one born among you, and you shall love him as yourself..."*

I was so caught up in their enthusiastic comradery that I was sorry to see the final hole. Their friend, Pat, birdied the 18th and we all got to scream, shout, high five, and knuckle knock! I was out of breath! But I was just following the advice to *"Rejoice with those who rejoice..."* (Romans 12:15).

Those three guys were the epitome of loyal and supportive friends. They waited for Pat and had lunch with him after the round. I sat at a distance, and loved watching them laugh, smile, and talk.

God is so faithful and loves us through others, especially when we choose to give. It is a choice!

I pray these examples motivate us to reach out in the spirit of friendship and give much more of ourselves to others, without any thought to what we will receive in return. This is how we demonstrate God's love, sharing from an overflow of a grateful heart.

Today, start "spreading the sugar!"

WHAT ARE WE THANKFUL FOR?

"Mom, I think it's time for me to get a dog!"

These were the words of our oldest, Brewer, not long ago. Actually, we had heard him say the same thing several years prior, when he was 17. And, yes, he got a dog!

I don't know what we were thinking! He was a senior in high school and I should have known the new puppy, "Daisy," was going to be *our* dog, and not Brewer's!

No regrets, Daisy has stolen our hearts.

So now, several years later, I drove with Brewer to pick up "his" new puppy, I wasn't at all worried that this would become *my* dog, since he is now on his own!

We were both absorbed in thinking of names and the anticipation of a new adventure! I was thrilled to be in on the journey and have our son in the car all to myself for three hours. Catching up and having one-on-one time, especially with the excitement we shared over the new addition, we talked non-stop!

In our family we are all animal lovers, especially dogs, and yellow labs in particular. So you could say we were both like children on Christmas Eve. To infer we were on "Cloud 9" would be an understatement!

By the time we drove up to the house of the new puppy, we were almost running to the front door. It was dark, but we could hear the dogs barking their greetings. The porch light was on and we entered the stranger's house. Two bulldogs met us and as we looked past them, there sat Brewer's new puppy with the cutest 16-month-old little boy—blonde hair and blue eyes, sitting next to him!

The puppy was precious, but what caught our attention even more was the "baby boy." This smiling and adorable little fellow immediately reached out his arms for me to pick him up, but the grandmother, who had opened the door, reached out for him instead, and placed him in a high chair. So we started playing on the floor with the puppy.

A minute later, we looked up at the child and noticed there was something very wrong with his feet. They were turned rather oddly. Seeing that we were staring, the grandmother proceeded to tell us her grandson had "spina bifida" and couldn't walk. She explained that she kept him while her daughter worked. "No day care would take him," she explained.

As she fed him yogurt, she began to pour out her heart about her grandson and daughter. When he finished eating, she put him back on the floor. Needless to say, our hearts went from being excited to being very heavy.

We sat for a while, playing with the puppy and watching how the dogs were very protective of the "precious baby."

It was late and we needed to drive home, so we finalized the paperwork and left. We did so with very mixed emotions.

While we were thankful for the puppy, our thoughts and prayers were now focused on a little boy who faced big challenges in his life. Never in a million years would I have counted on or foreseen how God would use "going to get a puppy" to soften and open our hearts to a stranger and her suffering grandchild.

The visual picture ingrained in my mind and in Brewer's, during the hour we spent in that house, was God's design to turn our hearts more toward the needs of others, even strangers! It also caused us to express our extreme gratitude over blessings we take for granted, such as the ability to walk.

I don't believe in coincidences, and we have made that child the continual focus of our prayers.

The moments of happiness we enjoy can take us by surprise. It is not that we seize them, but that they *seize us.* God never holds back—not in regards to a desire to show His love to others, taking a heart of stone and turning it to a "heart of flesh!"

GENEROSITY IS A FOREVER GIFT

"You can't outgive God!" I first heard this statement many years ago, but it still rings true and has been proven in my life over and over again.

I trust you have experienced it too, whether in the form of:

- A material gift
- A gift of service
- A listening ear
- An encouraging word
- A gift of forgiveness or grace

It's been said, "The poorest people in the world are the ones who do not give. Their thinking is so inward they choose to hold even their smiles."

Luke 12:48 reminds us, *"For everyone to whom much is given, from him much will be required; and to whom much has been committed, of him they will ask the more."*

God doesn't want us to catch the vision of *getting,* rather, the vision of *giving.*

Basketball coach John Wooden once stated, "You can't live a perfect day without doing something for someone who will never be able to repay you."

Our motivation should be giving without any thought of what we might receive in return. As it is written, *"All a person's ways seem pure to them, but motives are weighed by the Lord"* (Proverbs 16:2 NIV).

As a parent, some of the most rewarding moments have been when I have captured a glimpse of our kids giving without being asked, being generous from the overflow of their hearts. I relate this directly to how God must feel about me when I give, just to simply give.

There are countless gifts that I have received in my lifetime, as well as our family. At times, reminiscing over all of them puts a huge lump in my throat.

EXPRESSING GRATITUDE

On October 6, 2011, one of my dearest friends Sheryl Mayberry, said goodbye to her husband as he lost his brave battle with cancer. Bob, who owned successful automobile dealerships in Charlotte, North Carolina, understood what it meant to give without any expectation of return.

While at his funeral, I marveled at the tributes given concerning a life well lived, and listened intently at all he had done, especially for others, in the short span of 52 years.

This man, who we affectionately called "Moose," lived a full and busy life being a loving husband, father, son, brother, provider, and volunteer. Even though we did not reside in the same state, he still made time to be our friend and call just to see how we were doing.

His actions imprinted on my heart the desire to be a better friend, to be generous with the hours God gives me, and reach out to others. These are priceless gifts that will last, even after we have passed from this earth. This is why I celebrate the life of Bob Mayberry, who left me with the valuable and simple lesson of being generous.

Giving—it's our way of expressing gratitude.

NOTES FOR YOUR SCORECARD

- Be grateful for modern day Samaritans who come into your life.
- "Spread the Sugar" through unexpected acts of kindness.
- Give without any expectation of what you will receive.
- Be thankful when the Lord turns your attention to the needs of others.
- You can never outgive God.
- Giving includes, among other things, service, a listening ear, an encouraging word, and forgiveness.
- Be grateful for the priceless gift of love.

TEE #17
ENDURANCE

As I look back, I realize how much the Lord has developed my "courage muscle" and given me endurance through life's ups and downs.

Some experiences were painful and it took time before I was able to see the light at the end of the tunnel, but in the process the growth was unquestioned.

I pray that what I learned on a road that, at times, was filled with potholes and detours will give you strength for the challenges you face. On the next few pages we will see how our intentions and motives produce our actions and thoughts, the key to endurance, the results of fervent prayer, and how to find the power to forgive and bounce back from circumstances—including betrayal.

After being crowned Miss South Carolina, I immediately started making public appearances. The phone began ringing and my calender was soon filling up with speaking engagements at schools, churches, non-profit organizations, and corporations. I was asked to film Michelin Tire Corporate Videos, make commercials for a dairy company, and attend ribbon cutting ceremonies at stores and mall openings.

I remember packing my bags and preparing to go to an event in Myrtle Beach, South Carolina. It was a quick plane flight for an overnight event at a "journalism conference" where I was to be questioned by a panel of aspiring writers.

The Miss South Carolina Pageant Board saw this as an opportunity for me to hone my skills for the judge interviews at the upcoming "Miss America Pageant," which was just five weeks away.

Well, as you can imagine, I was new at this—a "sheep" on the way to the slaughter, you might say.

Calling these aspiring journalists *zealous* would be an understatement. They were ready for me, but I was not ready for them. I must admit, I had lived a rather sheltered life and was really not prepared for what was about to happen. Yes, I was an outspoken, unashamed Christian, and the reporters knew that. So, after being handed the microphone, the first question that was fired at me was, "Miss Thrift, what are your thoughts on abortion?"

I calmly and honestly replied, "I don't believe in abortion personally, and I support legal rights for the unborn child."

Well, that started the verbal onslaught, and for the next 45 minutes I felt like a raw piece of meat thrown into a pool of sharks that hadn't been fed in days. It was "electric chair" time, with a steady stream of high voltage questions that didn't kill me, but made me feel as if I couldn't breathe.

Sweating, I could feel the "burn" in every part of my body.

THE "COWBOY"

The panel questioning ended, and the ride back to the airport was a huge blur. But I'll never forget what happened when I boarded the plane. God was about to provide clarity in the form of a "cowboy."

I sat down next to a rather large male passenger. He was wearing Levi jeans, cowboy boots, a gigantic cowboy hat, and had a well-worn alligator briefcase resting on his lap. He stood up to let me scoot into the window seat next to him—a tight squeeze to say the least.

He must have seen the tears that were in my eyes, which felt like blood spatter to me, because with his big hand, he handed me a white handkerchief—a God thing for sure. He reminded me of my dad, who, to this day, doesn't use tissues, just cloth handkerchiefs.

I took it, but the tears kept flowing. My nose was running and his kind gesture made me wish my dad was actually there—and I sobbed some more.

After the plane took off and I became somewhat composed, the "cowboy" said, "Little darlin', would you like to tell me what has made that pretty face so sad?"

I looked up to see this smiling man and, through my tears, proceeded to tell this stranger of the "media attack!"

He listened intently, and at times patted my knee in a fatherly way. He asked me if he could share something with me, and I answered,"Yes, you may."

He proceeded to open his briefcase and pull out a "worn black Bible." Then he told me he was a college football coach and was leaving South Carolina after visiting a recruit and was headed back to Texas. I had no earthly idea who he was!

The coach proceeded to tell me he felt exactly as I did on the abortion issue! He then told me that courage was "to stand when no on else was standing."

And even though many people may not agree with me, the only one who mattered was God.

He applauded my courage, gave me some great tips on handling the media, and shared some personal stories from his own experience.

Then he opened the pages of his Bible to the story of David and Goliath, pointing to David's obvious fearlessness and his unlikely physical appearance to fight off the giant. He noted that David's bravery grew when he saw God's hand in his life after fighting off some wild animals.

He reminded me of David's words to Saul, *"Your servant has been keeping his father's sheep. When a lion or a bear came and carried off a sheep from the flock, I went after it, struck it and rescued the sheep from its mouth. When it turned on me, I seized it by its hair, struck it and killed it. Your servant has killed both the lion and the bear; this uncircumcised Philistine will be like one of them, because he has defied the armies of the living God"* (1 Samuel 17:34-36 NIV).

This coach told me that God was, in fact, preparing me for a bigger battle that lay ahead, competing for Miss America, a lifelong dream. Then he grabbed my hand, prayed and thanked God for His provision in helping me get ready to handle the press at the Miss America pageant.

He then advised: "Go home; ask God for wisdom on how to defend what you believe, and why. And never be ashamed of your beliefs, even if you are in the minority."

A DIVINE APPOINTMENT

When the plane landed, he gave me a hug, and we departed.

Suddenly, I realized that if he had told me his name, I didn't remember it. I called out, "Sir, could you please tell me your name?"

He took off his cowboy hat, extended his hand, and said, "I am Grant Teaff, head coach for the Baylor Bears. But to my friends and players I am called, Papa Bear. Please, Miss Thrift, call me Papa Bear."

He handed me his card and hugged me once again.

To me, this man was the Lord's hand extended. I wholeheartedly believe that God is sovereign. I have lived it, even though it required faith on my part before I saw the evidence.

The Lord knew what was in my future, even though I didn't. He allowed a very painful experience to be used for my greater good. In the process, He also provided a person to sooth my sorrow and bandage my wounds.

To this day I believe Coach Teaff (a dedicated Christian and head coach at Baylor for 22 years), was sitting next to me because the Lord orchestrated it. I later learned that Teaff, six-time Southwest Conference Coach of the Year, shares the same birthday as my earthly father.

The Lord knows the battles we will face, and will provide the strength to prepare us for tomorrow.

Corrie Ten Boom once said, "If God sends us on strong paths, we are provided strong shoes."

YOUR "HEART MUSCLE"

Our stamina and endurance starts deep on the inside.

The heart is a muscle the size of your fist, but it is

considered one of the "highest ranking organs" of the body. Its job is to pump oxygenated blood throughout the body from the top of our heads to the tips of our toes. This pumping action also sends the de-oxygenated blood back to the heart, which sends it to the lungs to be re-oxygenated (cleaned up) and then the process begins again.

The heart gets in trouble when there is a "blockage" that hinders the flow of blood. This can create many problems that affect the "whole body"—even life itself!

Science is very detailed regarding the physical understanding of the function and problems pertaining to the heart, and there have been phenomenal advances in medicine that help keep this vital organ healthy. However, what science doesn't address is the spiritual aspect of the heart, and its condition.

The Bible refers to the heart 830 times in 762 verses. Proverbs 27:19 tells us, *"As water reflects a face, so one's life reflects the heart"* (NIV).

YOUR TRUE TREASURE

Over 20 years ago, when Bill and I were introduced to a parenting Bible study called "Growing Kids God's Way," it stressed the importance of training our children's hearts—shaping their young lives by teaching them to understand Scripture and the "moral reason why" we are taught certain things.

For example, we whole-heartedly began teaching our kids at a young age the skill of "looking people in the eye" when they are talking to someone or being spoken to. There is no specific verse that addresses "eye contact," but when you are talking, this communicates your "value of them" and shows respect—a principle that *is* found throughout the Bible.

God's Word does directly address an area of the heart that is vital to carrying "oxygen" and keeping you healthy for your entire life. It is found in Matthew 22:37: *"Love the Lord your God with all your heart, with all your soul, and with all your mind."*

This act of love is given a higher priority than money or success—even above your feelings for your own *family.*

This is tough to swallow because, as a mother, I have to hold myself in check in order to keep my children from becoming idols in my life. But anything is considered an idol if it comes before God. As Jesus points out, *"Where your treasure is, there your heart will be also"* (Luke 12:34).

So in order to fulfill "loving God with all my heart," I have to daily check what I truly treasure. After all, I can veer onto the wrong path, as they say, in a "skinny minute!"

ENDURANCE FOR THE RACE

Growing up, and to this day, one of the most helpful and meaningful passages of Scripture to me is reading what God said to Samuel when he was charged with finding a king to replace Saul. God reminded Samuel that in his quest, *"Man looks at the outward appearance, but the Lord looks at the heart"* (1 Samuel 16:7).

God sees our intent and motives, which drive all of our actions and thoughts! This is sobering, because we live in a world that promotes the visible exterior, rather than the invisible interior.

We are even told, *"For out of the abundance* [overflow] *of the heart the mouth speaks"* (Matthew 12:34).

This convicts me, and daily I have to make an inward evaluation to see if I have a blockage that could trigger a "spiritual heart attack!"

This requires stopping to think about my words, which reflect my actions.

Even more significant is the fact that our thoughts precede our behavior; so it all starts in the heart and mind.

In the physical we worry over our health and developing "hardening of the arteries," but God has a spiritual solution. He promises: *"I will give you a new heart and put a new spirit in you. I will remove from you your heart of stone and give you a heart of flesh"* (Ezekiel 36:26).

This is how the Lord gives you strength, not only to compete, but to win. We are told: *"Let us run with endurance the race that is set before us, looking unto Jesus, the author and finisher of our faith, who for the joy that was set before Him endured the cross, despising the shame, and has sat down at the right hand of the throne of God"* (Hebrews 12:1-2).

YOUR "INNER DRIVE"

Endurance certainly doesn't come from sitting around, twiddling your thumbs. Being lazy not only depletes your energy, but can often lead to painful consequences! Just open your Bible, turn to the book of Proverbs, and highlight how many verses refer to this topic. Here are just a few:

- *"He who has a slack hand becomes poor, but the hand of the diligent makes rich"* (Proverbs 10:4).

- *"The hand of the diligent will rule, but the lazy man will be put to forced labor"* (Proverbs 12:24).
- *"In all labor there is profit, but idle chatter leads only to poverty"* (Proverbs14:23).
- *"The lazy man will not plow because of winter; he will beg during harvest and have nothing"* (Proverbs 20:4).
- *"Do not sleep, lest you come to poverty; open your eyes, and you will be satisfied with bread"* (Proverbs 20:13).

I am so very grateful to have grown up with parents who had a strong work ethic. My mom never slowed down until failing health forced her to. And dad spent most of his life going to work at 5:30 AM every morning, even putting in hours on Saturdays if necessary. He took one week off, around the Fourth of July, and a few days at Christmas—and that was it. It baffled and annoyed him in equal measures when he had an employee who would "lay out of work sick"—only to later learn they had been seen around town, perfectly fit, doing other things.

It was rare if my sister and I ever slept in on Saturday morning. Dad would breeze into the bedroom and say," "You can't sleep the day away!" I think he wrestled with the fear that we could grow up and be lazy.

Living through the depression, my father knew what it was like to be hungry—and never wanted his daughters to have such an experience. Even though he didn't have the privilege of attending college, he insisted on it for his girls. More than once he told us, "I'll only pay for your wedding if you graduate from college." Both of us honored his wish.

He also strongly emphasized that an education would not

automatically make us successful, saying, "Success comes from "an inward drive and a strong work ethic!" In addition, he told us, "Even though your education isn't going to cost you anything, nothing is free. Someone else has to work to pay for it."

With our own children, we allowed them to pursue their dreams of earning their college tuition through athletics. This was something foreign to me, but not to their dad, who had achieved this through a football scholarship. Even though golf is a game, it is actually the "work" they put in that produced the finances for their tuition. This is true for young people who earn either an academic or athletic scholarship.

A strong work ethic can be instilled and learned in many ways—hard labor, diligent study, skill development, practicing a talent, etc.

The most important detail is to realize that the Lord requires us to *work*, regardless of what we choose to do.

We should take the words of Paul the Apostle to heart: *"Whatever you do, do it heartily, as to the Lord and not unto men"* (Colossians 3:23).

It is this attribute that produces vitality, perseverance, and endurance.

STAY AWAKE!

To me, one of the saddest, heart-wrenching stories in the Bible is the night before Jesus was to be crucified—and He *knew* what was waiting ahead. Christ went to the Garden of Gethsemane to pray and asked the disciples to keep watch, only to return an hour later and find them sleeping. He requested this of them three times, and on each occasion they promised they would, yet fell asleep.

Jesus was in such anguish that He sweat "drops of blood" while talking with His Father. There are three accounts of this in Scripture (Matthew 26:36-46, Luke 22:39-46, and Mark 14:32-42).

Of all people, the disciples were closest to Jesus. They believed, followed, and lived with Him, yet in His hour of need, when He asked them to watch and pray, they slept.

The disciples were faithful friends, but weak humans. To be honest, most of us could not pull an all-nighter on our knees!

We may see ourselves as disciples of Christ, but often we are guilty of closing our eyes to a friend who is in anguish.

Down through the years the Lord has shown me that I can't be all things to all people, but I should be able to pray anywhere, anytime. It doesn't have to be fancy, long, or eloquent, yet it must be *sincere*. It doesn't matter if the person is aware I am praying for them or not, as long as Jesus knows.

I love "arrow prayers"—shot directly to God on behalf of others. I also value the fact that they shoot them for me—because the Lord hears every one of them. The Bible tells us, *"The effective, fervent prayer of a righteous man avails much"* (James 5:16). The Son of God prayed, *"Father, if it is Your will, take this cup away from me; nevertheless not My will, but Yours, be done"* (Luke 22:42).

As believers, we talk to the Lord, knowing He hears our prayers, and that they are important to Him and avail much.

However, we must leave the answer up to the will of God—trusting Him to work and act according to His good purpose, even though we may not understand.

The power of prayer gives us endurance to face any test.

BOUNCING BACK FROM BETRAYAL

I don't need to conduct a survey to know that by the time you reach the Back Nine of life, at some point you have experienced the knife of betrayal.

When it happens because of the actions of a friend, it seems far worse—often producing extreme hurt, shock, anger, and feelings of despair and loneliness.

One of the hardest days for a mom is to watch your child experience this for the first time. Perhaps it is as simple as seeing one of their close buddies join a clique at school —leaving them on the outside. Or being told, "I don't like you anymore." As adults, we can face the same issue because of workplace envy, an unscrupulous business partner, or an unfaithful spouse.

There is no Advil, Tylenol, word, or hug that quickly soothes the pain. It is a slow recovery; something only time, prayer, and God can help us heal from.

Playwrite Arthur Miller observed, "Betrayal is the only truth that sticks." I like to change that last word to "stinks" —because it really does.

When someone has felt this sharp knife, my mind

immediately turns to what happened to Jesus because of one of His disciples, Judas.

Think of it! Judas was considered a close friend and follower of Jesus. Today he would be described as being in the "inner circle"—so much so that he was trusted to carry the "money bag" during the travels of Christ (see John 12:4-6).

Just before the crucifixion, Judas betrayed Jesus for money. He went to the chief priests and asked, *"'What are you willing to give me if I deliver Him to you?' And they counted out to him thirty pieces of silver. So from that time he sought opportunity to betray Him"* (Matthew 26:15-16).

The sources of such treachery are usually self-gain or jealousy, as depicted in the Old Testament story of Jacob's son, Joseph. After Joseph told his dream to his brothers, Scripture records that they *"envied him"* (Genesis 37:11).

They were so consumed with jealousy that they conspired to kill him, but eventually decided to throw him into a pit. Then they chose to sell him as a slave and lie to their father to cover up their conspiracy. In Egypt, Joseph was further betrayed by Potiphar's wife (see Genesis 39).

When you read these stories, they seem unthinkable, but sellouts of this nature even happen today. To ease the pain, some turn to drugs or alcohol, but they are no real fix. Only in calling on a Higher Power can we rise above the betrayal and reach a point of forgiveness.

I love the above accounts Scripture has given us to learn from—Jesus and Joseph! Christ is the ultimate example of what it means to forgive after being betrayed. Following His death and resurrection He even restored Peter, another member of Jesus' inner circle, who denied Him three times after Christ's arrest.

Being human, there are emotions that accompany betrayal. The Bible gives us a glimpse of Joseph's feelings when it speaks of how, when he saw his brothers after years of separation, *"he turned himself away from them and wept"* (Genesis 42:24).

This teaches me that this sin can be forgiven, but its pain can linger for years.

Because of God's principle of sowing and reaping, the betrayer suffers as well. In the case of Judas, after Jesus' arrest, he was filled with remorse, threw the money back to the priests and, in despair, hung himself.

And when we look at the story of Joseph, we read of the anguish some of his brothers lived with for years because of their actions.

The consequences of the betrayal of Jesus served to save mankind from eternal damnation. And the selling out of Joseph, in the end, saved his family from starvation.

BOUNCING BACK FROM DISAPPOINTMENT

"Show me Your ways, Lord, teach me Your paths" (Psalm 25:4).

Thomas was wearing the "coat of disappointment" as he came home from Q School in late fall, 2014 (Q stands for Qualifying).He was quiet and meek, sad over his play and not making it to the next stage of Q School—one way to get your "Tour card." It would have put him one step closer to his dream of playing on the PGA tour. Thomas has dreamed, since around the age of 10, of playing at that level.

If you are not a golfer, let me summarize the importance of Q School for you. It starts every fall and ends in December and is composed of four tournaments. You have to make the cut in all tournaments or stages in order to make it to the final stage. Then you have to make the Top 25 to be qualified to play in "Tour" (professional events). Q School isn't the only way to "skin the cat," but it is one way. Now that door was closed for Thomas until the next September.

We have all learned to pray and remain silent after major disappointments in our house. Silent until the one who is "down" is ready to talk and process it with someone else. So, when Thomas arrived home, I knew I had to wait. It wasn't until a week later that Thomas appeared in my study one morning to start talking through his hurts and disappointments. I had been praying months in advance over our son's future—for direction, endurance, vision, provision, and God's confirmation. I also prayed for my words and advice to him as he worked to "pursue his dream!" I can honestly say through prayer, and prayer alone, do I feel God has confirmed that Thomas' dream is from God.

As our son has grown, he has never wavered in his work ethic, no matter the outcomes. He graduated from college in four years and finished strong. He made the Dean's List his last semester, when most kids check out. He, on many occasions, has shared his thoughts. I have prayed specifically asking the Lord to guide his steps, to direct our advice to him, and asked for God's provision.

Being 52 as I write this, and still pursuing dreams and goals that the Lord placed in my heart at an early age, I am more than aware that following and seeking God in all things is the only path to take.

I have come to understand God directs us in unique and individual ways. Sometimes the route on which we find ourselves is not the norm. He does this simply so we can see Him more clearly.

As we navigate these paths, confirmation comes and there is no doubt it is of God and not of ourselves.

Obviously, we need to mature and be prepared to handle the road of our dreams, because Big Dreams fulfilled can come with Big Responsibility—the kind we can't always imagine or prepare for since we have never walked that way before. There are many reasons, and they vary, as to why God does what He does. I will be the first to admit that often in this life the future may not be made clear to us. But He is directing us and we are developing endurance.

AN UNEXPECTED TURN

A week after Thomas came home from not making the cut to go to the next stage of Q School, Mike, our daughter's boyfriend, *did* make it. He asked Thomas to travel with him to Florida and be his caddy. Thomas did not hesitate. In my spiritual walk with Christ, I have learned that serving others is a true blessing, especially if you have really nothing to gain. Well, Thomas had nothing to gain except time spent with Mike. They are great friends outside of Mike's and Collins' relationship.

Two days after Thomas and Mike arrived in Florida, I sent a simple text asking how things were going. Thomas texted, "It is good…but this is very humbling. I so wish I could be where Mike is, but that is just not God's plan."

I encouraged him by saying, "Embrace the humble place. Scripture teaches that is when God can do His best work in our lives." I also told him that when you do things for others, out of the goodness of your heart, God brings favor. And I reminded him that we do things "just because"—and not to look for blessings. But usually God's economy works like this: He blesses a servant's heart and one who endures.

Thomas texted, "Ok. Thanks mom!" That was it.

Four hours later I received another text from Thomas, "Mom…guess what?"

Let me pause here and say that when Thomas texts or says to me, "Guess what?" he is about to share a God moment.

He then told me, "I just got a text from Jordan Byrd letting me know a Clemson donor and alumni has offered me a spot in the E-Golf Tour Championship in Hilton Head on December 3-6."

Most guys in that Championship had to earn their way there from their play throughout the year. A few others who get in are offered "sponsor's exemptions." Thomas read about the tournament online but didn't even try to get in because he hadn't played that tour all year. The invitation was an out of the blue gift! Thomas currently didn't have any status that warranted him getting in. I hope you are understanding or seeing the "God moment." Thomas texted asking if I thought he should take it. I responded, "Absolutely. This is from the Lord!"

Fast forward a bit. God provided a free place to stay in

Hilton Head with dear Christian friends, Dana and Gerrick Taylor. The Lord also worked in the hearts of my dad and uncle to give Brewer time off from work to caddy for Thomas. God allowed Thomas to have success—finishing 13 out of a field of 175 players. He even earned money!

You see, I had been praying for God to encourage our son in a direction so that there would be no doubt as to the road he should take. This was confirmed by the "gift of the invitation!"

Funny, a side benefit and message from God to Thomas I feel is this: "I have you, Thomas. Follow me. It all doesn't have to be in your strength. Work hard but rest in Me and allow Me to take you down My path. Humility, trust, and having a servant's heart is key. That is a man God can use!"

We can all benefit from that message!

Psalm 18:36 reminds us that our heavenly Father is giving us strength and direction: *"You provide a broad path for my feet, so that my ankles do not give way."* God enables endurance.

We certainly don't know what tomorrow holds, but we know the One who does. His ways are not our ways. Our job is to be faithful and seek God with all our heart and in all our actions, knowing we will fall short at times. That is where God's grace covers and we just repent and keep moving down the path that God promises to light as we walk behind Him, not in front!

"Your word is a lamp for my feet, a light on my path" (Psalm 119:105).

NOTES FOR YOUR SCORECARD

- The Lord will send people into your life to give you courage to endure.
- We must develop both our physical and spiritual "heart muscle."
- Our intents and motives produce our actions and thoughts.
- God will give you the strength to run "with endurance."
- Your inner drive is the key to endurance.
- Fervent prayers are effective, and allow us to face any test.
- We may be betrayed, but the Lord will give us the power to forgive and bounce back.

Tee #18
Victory!

Since going public with "Back 9 Ministries" there have been a few surprises I didn't see on the horizon. During these past years I have come to understand, at a very deep level, that when you obey God fully, you can also *trust* Him completely. I can tell you from personal experience that He will guide, counsel, protect, teach, grow and bless you all at the same time.

On this final tee, there are several principles I want to share with you, including: how to "strike oil" in your own backyard, the fact that the design of the Creator is not for just certain individuals, but for YOU, and how to experience what it means to give your "all." We will also focus on leaving a spiritual legacy for your children and the awesome rewards of running the race and finishing strong.

When Peter climbed out of the boat to walk on the water toward Jesus—he was only safe from drowning when he kept his eyes fixed on the Lord. When the disciple glanced away, he started to sink.

I now know beyond doubt that when we totally trust the Lord and obey His directives, He is in control of all outcomes—and we are not. And, in order to fully obey, our "eye contact" with Him has to be steadfast and constant.

Perhaps you have heard it said, "God doesn't call the equipped, He equips the called!" This definitely describes me!

I can now appreciate that God furnished me a long time

ago with certain talents, gifts, parents, family, husband, kids, friends, and experiences that have all worked together for what He has called me to do in the "Back Nine" of life.

However, in my commitment to this ministry, the Lord has let me know that by myself, I am inadequate—and that I am balancing on a "tightrope."

Perhaps you remember watching the live television coverage of Nick Wallenda crossing a 1,500-foot gorge of the Grand Canyon on a tightrope—without a net!

On my journey, I realize I need to look straight ahead, not to the left, right, up, down, or behind me. I can do this with the assurance that God is my safety net! He has me taking just one step at a time, all the while keeping my focus on *Him*.

THE ADVENTURE

People ask, "Sherry, where is your ministry headed?" I wish I had all the answers, but one thing is for sure: to reach where I am today has been a long process, and I have to get up every morning to prayerfully seek God's face, listening for His leading. I know that I am to encourage others to lead a life of significance, and it is awesome how the Lord opens doors one after another to see His purpose for me fulfilled.

When I felt the urge to start writing a blog on our website, I wasn't sure that it was truly God speaking. Honestly, I didn't think I had the time or natural ability to do such a thing, and in truth, I don't. But I began the blog anyway. It's been quite an adventure. Sometimes when I write and go back later and read my entries, I am shocked and amazed. There were days when I had no memory of what I had written! All I can conclude is that it must be God equipping me.

Please don't get me wrong, The stories are true and as accurate as God allows me to remember. (But there are days when I crawl into bed and can't even recall what I ate for breakfast.) However, when I go back and read, it's just what the Lord wanted me to say.

In addition, since I am a recovering "people pleaser," I was warned by a small group of friends who hold me accountable, not to get too caught up in the positive or negative feedback from readers. Well, in a way, the affirming reaction has been surprising, especially since I went overboard preparing myself for criticism. In the past, my reaction to negativity has kept me bouncing around like a ping pong ball, trying to please others rather than the Lord.

So the nice comments have filled my tank to overflowing, something I really hadn't planned on. The kind responses have been hugs from God.

Even though I was at first anxious, I decided to be obedient and tell the Lord, "I will trust You." His blessings have arrived in unexpected ways.

A wonderful bonus has been God's provision of people to assist me. With a business degree, I have always been a firm believer that you are only as good and successful as the people with whom you surround yourself. The team that God assembled (and how) has been beyond any expectations. They came together smoothly as a result of prayer—and me not trying to run ahead of the Lord as I have been so guilty of doing in the past.

In the process, I learned to "drop my hands" so God could drive my life. He definitely does a masterful job, and has demonstrated this in every aspect of launching the ministry.

THE FAITH WALK

Has everything been a breeze? Hardly! Just before starting my blog, Satan launched an attack, as he always does against anyone trying to please God.

The devil hit me hard, by emotionally attacking one of our children, and causing a detour in their plans. Remember, mothers have an invisible umbilical cord, and what happens to her child is also felt by her.

At the time, this took over my heart and attention. But greater is He who is in me (and that child) than He who is in the world. Looking back, we see that what Satan meant for evil, God is making not just good, but great!

We cannot control Satan's onslaught, but we can trust the Lord. Walking by faith and not by sight is the only way to live.

Listen to the words of Your heavenly Father when He promises, *"You will seek Me and find Me, when you seek me with all your heart. I will be found by you"* (Jeremiah 29:13-14).

There is no secret in finding God and all that He has for you; simply search for Him. I have proven it again and again that you can trust Him to equip, protect, guide, and take you to places you could never go in your own strength.

The old saying is still true: *If you want to walk on water, you have to get out of the boat!"*

STRIKING OIL

What if you were told from a reputable source that hidden somewhere in your backyard was oil, and if you drilled you would strike it rich? With such information, I'm sure you would find the time to explore the possibilities.

At the price of oil, if I hit a gusher, it would certainly be profitable—and our backyard would look a whole lot different! But in reality, how much would I have to invest upfront to do this? Remember, I already knew the oil was there; I just had to go dig for it!

In one respect, this same concept is true for everyone. God blessed each of us with gifts—"oil"—to be drilled for and discovered. But far too often we choose to either doubt or ignore, and don't put forth the effort to discover what we already have!

For years now, I have known that God has favored me with the gift of encouragement, then one day, in a quiet moment, He revealed that it was time for me to "step it up." More clearly, the Lord impressed upon my heart that I needed to drill—to use my spiritual gift to write a book.

In the past, this was used on a daily basis, one-on-one, to find ways to lift the spirits of others, but now God was telling me to "drill deep" through the process of writing!

To be honest, the thought was "overwhelming"—a word that has defined many areas of my life in the last several years. I started looking for excuses, worrying, *I have never done anything like this before: Where do I begin? How do I write a whole book? Who will advise and help me? And where would I find a publisher?*

This was way out of my realm of expertise; I was totally unfamiliar with being an author, or even who to call for advice. But over a period of several months, the fire within me to write/drill became so apparent that I could no longer close my eyes or ignore the prompting.

This resulted in my first book, *The Front Nine*.

THE NEXT LEVEL

We *all* have "gifts/oil" in our own backyard that the Lord wants us to tap into in order to serve one another.

God's desire is not exclusive to certain individuals—it's for everyone, including YOU!

You may have discovered your gift and are using it in a small way as opportunities arise. Have you ever considered that the Lord wants you to take it up a notch—even multiplying your potential?

As we read in the story of the "talents" in Matthew 25, God expects us to increase what we have been given according to our ability. And in 1 Peter 4:10 we read, *"Each of you should use whatever gift you have received to serve others, as faithful stewards of God's grace in its various forms"* (NIV).

I pray you can see by my own example that regardless of your age or lack of experience it is never too late. Take time to find a quiet place before a Holy God and "strike oil" to serve and fuel others. In my case, it took a willingness to listen, a boldness to step out, and a decision to trust and obey—and the Lord has provided every step of the way.

Some things require "sweat," and moving out of a comfort zone. I had to acquire a discipline and commitment to drilling—leaving the results to the Lord.

I challenge you to ask God today to reveal your gifts. If you already know them, ask how you can drill deeper to provide for the needs of those around you.

Finally, roll up your sleeves, step out, and start walking. If the Lord came through for me; He will certainly do the same for you. Remember, *"There are diversities of gifts, but the same Spirit. There are differences of ministries, but the same Lord. And there are diversities of activities, but it is the same God who works all in all"* (1 Corinthians 12:4-6).

What has the Lord asked of you?

A CELEBRATION IN HEAVEN

Life has a way of coming full circle. My mom has been a rock in our family for as long as I can remember—solid, strong, trustworthy, and dependable. But the day came when her physical strength began to weaken. Over time, it reached the point where she needed help with basic daily routines. Then, in the spring of 2014, we knew, even before the doctors confirmed our fears, that her life was drawing to a close.

As the final days approached, the Lord soothed my spirit as I sat by her bed, along with my dad and sister, our spouses and kids. We watched her suffer in silence and await her call to be with the Lord. He provided this time for us to prepare our hearts for her departure and we were comforted in knowing that we would be reunited with her one day.

Through the process of the gradual loss of my mother, I realized how much I had to be thankful for.

As Christians, we believe that God's timing is perfect—and it is!

I am truly grateful that our entire family was able to hold her hand, love on her in her sleep, and tell her a long and heartfelt goodbye. The nurses told me she could hear our voices, even though in the last hours there was little evidence that she could.

Her grandchildren, nieces, and nephews came into her room independently of each other, and she would open her eyes or raise her eyebrows when she heard their voices. I was able to witness some of those cherished moments.

Watching my father grieve over my mother tore at my heartstrings. I had never felt such pain, nor had I seen Dad weep so—telling her again and again how much he loved her.

In the book of Ecclesiastes we are told, *"For everything there is a season, a time for every purpose under heaven: a time to be born, and a time to die...a time to weep, and a time to laugh; a time to mourn, and a time to dance"* (Ecclesiastes, 3:1-2,4).

Our mourning is ongoing, because the loss has been deep and wide. Mom was everything God instructs a mother to be. Yet I know there was a joyous celebration in heaven on April 16, 2014, when she traded her earthly home for a mansion that was awaiting her. For my mom, this was a time of great victory.

My desire is for my children to be left with such a rich legacy.

SHE GAVE HER ALL

If I were asked to rate my favorite stories in Scripture, the following would definitely be in my top five. Even if you are not a Bible reader, you should turn to the account of the "widow's offering" in Luke 21. It is a story of true love.

At the temple in Jerusalem, Jesus noticed the rich and privileged bringing their gifts to the treasury. He also saw a very poor woman put two small copper coins in the offering. Touched by her generosity, He stated, *"Truly I say to you that this poor widow has put in more than all; for all these out of their abundance have put in offerings for God, but she out of her poverty put in all the livelihood that she had"* (verses 3-4).

This tender story speaks to my heart. Here was a woman who was all alone, down to the last coins she needed for survival, and yet she gave her *all* to God's house, out of her love for the Lord.

I've heard people speculate on who they want to see when they walk through the Pearly Gates. Of course, I can hardly wait to see my mom, and other loved ones who have gone before me. But I also want to meet that widow—and I'll have plenty of questions to ask her: "How did your husband die? Did you have children? Tell me about your personal testimony. What events led you to bring the last of your earthly possessions to God's house?"

Actually, this selfless act at the temple makes me feel somewhat ashamed. Have I made the ultimate sacrifice? Have I given everything to the Lord?

Like most people, I'm still a work in progress, earnestly seeking to know and love Christ more every day. And I long for others to know God's grace and over-flowing abundance that can only be experienced through a personal relationship with Him.

If it sounds simple to know Jesus, it *is!* It makes no difference to your heavenly Father what you have done in the past, your background, or the possessions you may have accumulated. All that is needed is a mustard seed of faith to believe He exists and have a sincere desire to know Him—all the while trusting and inviting Him to come into your heart and be the Lord of your life. He will! I promise!

From a young age, I have never been ashamed of the "Gospel"—which means the story of Jesus; His life, His death, and His resurrection.

The one thing that no one can ever dispute is my personal testimony of what Christ has done for and through me! That is why my belief is so unshakable. I have a first-hand account of what the Lord has done—and no one can argue with that.

A SIMPLE PRAYER

If you are reading this and have never accepted Christ as

your Savior, I invite you to pray this simple prayer with me:

Dear Lord Jesus, I know that I am a sinner, and I ask for Your forgiveness. I believe You died for my sins and rose from the dead. I turn from my sins and invite You to come into my heart and life. I want to trust and follow You as my Lord and Savior. In Your Name. Amen.

These words, prayed with sincerity, will make an eternal difference. The Lord will become real to you. This is not just a promise from me, but from God's holy Word: *"If you confess with your mouth the Lord Jesus and believe in your heart that God has raised Him from the dead, you will be saved. For with the heart one believes unto righteousness, and with the mouth confession is made unto salvation"* (Romans 10:9-10).

Welcome to the family of God!

FINISH STRONG

In this game called life, all of us will reach the last inning, the final quarter, or the 18th "green."

In golf, I have always encouraged our kids to "finish strong!" I know how vital this is—and it is a biblical principle.

Once, Jesus told a large crowd that was following Him, *"For which of you, intending to build a tower, does not sit down first and count the cost, whether he has enough to finish it—lest, after he has laid the foundation, and is not able to finish, all who see it begin to mock him, saying, 'This man began to build and was not able to finish'"?* (Luke 14:28-30).

This race is not for quitters. As Paul the Apostle wrote, *"But one thing I do: forgetting what is behind and straining toward what is ahead, I press on toward the goal to win the prize for which God has called me heavenward in Christ Jesus"* (Philippians 3:13-14 NIV).

The Lord told the church at Sardis to *"strengthen the things which remain"* (Revelation 3:2).

Our eternal rewards are not based on the beginning of our race, but the ending: "He who overcomes shall inherit all things" (Revelation 10:7).

YOU'RE ABOUT TO WIN!

Fulfilling God's will is a desire the Lord has placed deep within me. This means taking all I have learned and experienced so far and investing my time to do more—and live a life worth duplicating.

I'm fully aware that I cannot accomplish this in my own power, I rely on the fact that *"I can do all things through Christ who strengthens me"* (Philippians 4:13).

On our course, God gives grace along the way as we learn and mature. The Lord longs for us to complete the particular task He has chosen.

When the Apostle Paul, perhaps the greatest missionary of

all time, was nearing the end of his earthly journey, he wrote these words to his son in the ministry, young Timothy: *"I have fought the good fight, I have finished the race, I have kept the faith"* (2 Timothy 4:7).

As we are about to pull the flag on the final hole, the Lord wants us to show what it means to demonstrate the perseverance and maturity of a true champion. This is why we are counseled, *"Let patience have its perfect work, that you may be perfect and complete, lacking nothing"* (James 1:4).

The conflict can be tough at times, but we have been equipped with supernatural battle gear that allows us to *"be strong in the Lord and in the power of His might"* (Ephesians 6:10).

We are to put on the armor of God, that we may be able to *"stand against the wiles of the devil. For we do not wrestle against flesh and blood, but against principalities, against powers, against the rulers of the darkness of this age, against spiritual hosts of wickedness in the heavenly places. Therefore take up the whole armor of God, that you may be able to withstand in the evil day, and having done all, to stand"* (verses 11-13).

Thankfully, in this battle we are being led by a Warrior, a General, who has already defeated the enemy—His name is Jesus. Because of this, the last chapter in the life of every believer has been written. We win!

Victory is within your reach!

NOTES FOR YOUR SCORECARD

- Trust God. What the enemy means for evil, the Lord means for good.
- You can "strike oil" in your own backyard.
- The design of the Creator is not for just certain individuals—it's for YOU!
- Make it your desire to leave a spiritual legacy for your children.
- Experience what it means to give your "all."
- Make the decision to finish strong.
- The crown of life is yours when you fight the good fight, finish the race, and keep the faith!

BEFORE YOU PUT YOUR CLUBS IN THE BAG

Thus far, my life experiences have taught me:

1. To have a poise that is more unshakable than panic.
2. To own what I believe and defend it.
3. An appreciation for discipline and a strong work ethic over a passion for leisure. Proverbs 6:6: *"Go to the ant, you sluggard; consider its ways and be wise!"*
4. That first impressions matter!
5. To understand it is not about me. When you walk into a room, it is not "Here I am," but "There you are!" It is very true that people really don't care about what you know until they know you care.
6. Being *real* is important as is being transparent. People are, in general, very smart. Being fake and robotic is not appreciated or valued.

7. To be me is good enough, but *being* me has to be a work in progress—always seeking to grow and improve and being a better version of myself daily. We may stop growing physically, but never mentally. We have to choose to be a lifelong learner. As John Wooden said, "If you choose not to be a lifelong reader, you choose a life of ignorance."
8. The importance of being teachable—understanding in every situation you are in, that you can learn if you choose to. *"For wisdom will enter your heart, and knowledge will be pleasant to your soul"* (Proverbs 2:10 NIV).
9. That everyone doesn't have your greater good in mind—so be gentle as a dove and wise as a serpent. I place a higher value on people's actions than I do on their words (see Matthew 10:16).
10. When you lose, you win. Losing is a great teacher.
11. Jealousy is real, but don't focus on it. It's not my/your problem unless you are the jealous one, then kill the monster before it kills you!
12. "People pleasing" can take you completely off the path your heavenly Father has planned for you! "God pleasing" is the ultimate choice for anyone's life. *"Am I now trying to win the approval of human beings, or of God? Or am I trying to please people? If I were still trying to please people, I would not be a servant of Christ"* (Galatians 1:10 NIV).
13. Lean heavily into the evaluated experience of others; men and women who have "been there and done that"—*"...turning your ear to wisdom and your heart to understanding"* (Proverbs 2:2 NIV).

14. Out of the overflow of the heart the mouth speaks. It's better to have a good heart. If you don't, you won't be able to hide it. You can choose to be a polluter (toxic) or a pollinator (nourishing). It is a choice.
15. The media is like a cat—finicky—rubbing on your leg one minute and scratching you the next. Whatever sells. So don't get too caught up in their hype.
16. There is no reward without risk—or no crown without competing.
17. People identify more with your losses/adversity than your wins.
18. Your past shapes you, but your actions define you.
19. Life is like a rubber band: it is only useful when it is "stretched." Live out of your comfort zone.
20. Life is a stage. It is a continual runway—with a spotlight. A friend, wife/husband, mother/father, job/career, volunteer, son/daughter, aunt/uncle —someone is always watching.

God gives each of us potential; our gift back to Him is to develop it. *"But in fact God has placed the parts in the body, every one of them, just as he wanted them to be"* (1 Corinthians 12:18).

The sun may be setting, but make sure you are always looking for *Possibilities,* keeping a positive *Attitude,* pursuing the right *Objectives,* making a total *Commitment,* providing *Encouragement* to others, maintaining *Determination,* expressing *Gratitude,* and praying for *Endurance.*

On *The Back Nine* of life, you're ready for *Victory!*

To Schedule the Author
for Speaking Engagements, Contact:
www.Back9Ministries.org